Fabulous Fit

Judith Rasband

Fairchild Publications New York

ISBN: 87005-739-1

Library of Congress Catalog Card Number: 92-73505

GST R133004424

Printed in the United States of America

This book is dedicated to the memory of Martha Jo Martin.

I was privileged to meet Dr. Martha Jo Martin in 1989 at the annual meeting of the American Home Economics Association. Learning of my illness, she took precious time to introduce herself to me as one who had experienced breast cancer and chemotherapy. Her very positive attitude and helpful information, coupled with letters and calls during the months that followed were a source of strength and coping skills throughout my own treatment and recovery. With recurring illness, Dr. Martha Jo Martin passed away in 1990. A devoted wife, mother and home economist, she will be sincerely missed.

Contents

Preface

My seatmate on the plane was reclining and reading a best-selling spy novel. I know. I peeked. I was sitting upright with my lap tray down. I was cutting, snipping and taping quarter-scale paper patterns. I noticed that every once in a while, my seatmate would sneak a peek in my direction.

Finally, curiosity won out. He closed his book and said to me, "It looks like you're enjoying your second childhood, but I suspect you're working with something more technical than paper dolls. What are you doing anyway?"

"I'm altering patterns," I replied. "I'm trying to decide on the easiest and most effective way to get clothes to fit—depending on the figure variation, of course."

"The figure what?" he queried. And that launched us into a conversation that lasted right up until landing. He voiced his own frustration in trying to find collars, sleeves and pants that fit. He told me about every figure variation and fitting problem for every member of his family. He took home altered patterns for his wife and two daughters. He even had a handful for the tailor to try when next he bought a suit for himself or his son.

My own awareness of the frustration people feel when they try to get clothes that fit and flatter escalated with my first teaching position. Students struggled to select styles that would camouflage areas of their figures they'd just as soon the world didn't notice.

Even after selecting a seemingly suitable style, the student often had to alter the pattern to fit. At that point, someone inevitably came to me to complain, "Mrs. Rasband, this method doesn't work." Time after time I had to agree. But I had nothing better to offer.

I struggled myself, to refine or improve on traditional concepts, strategies and methods—to eliminate distortions inherent with the methods. With each new teaching position I worked to develop new ways of stating concepts, new ways to outline strategies—ways that were appealing, practical, easy to understand and apply; ways that would help students gain the skill and confidence they needed. Many of the concepts, strategies and methods I came to depend on in the classroom and in the consumer marketplace are included in this book.

The problem of pattern alteration was most maddening. In a fit of frustration, I one day exclaimed to my colleague, "This alteration for broad shoulders absolutely does not work! Look at the distortion."

"Try this," she offered. And with a couple of cuts on the pattern, she left for her class. I looked. I wiggled the paper. It worked. And without the usual distortion. What was this creative innovation? And why weren't we all using it?

That was just the beginning. I cut, snipped and taped for weeks. If the seam method, as I had begun to call it, worked in one place, I hoped it would work in others as well. Results confirmed my expectations and were well received by students and several colleagues alike.

This innovative seam method of alteration was certainly worth testing and the project was approved for my masters thesis. The published thesis results were reported at the 1978 annual meeting of the Association of College Professors of Textiles and Clothing (now named the International Textiles and Apparel Association).

Convinced others would be equally enthusiastic about the seam method of alteration, I had outlined the plan for a textbook. It was an overwhelming project and because of her own work in pattern drafting and alteration, Elizabeth Liechty joined me in collaborating on the book. We later invited Della Pottberg to join us and, together, we completed the manuscript during after-hours over the next five years. Titled *Fitting and Pattern Alteration: A Multi-Method Approach*, the text includes a detailed discussion of three methods of alteration, applied to 85 figure variations. The traditional slash method was corrected and included with the pivot method, in part, for the benefit of individuals already familiar with them. Both methods produce the same accurate results as the new and innovative seam method.

Response to *Fitting and Pattern Alteration* has been outstanding. Students, home sewers, seminar patrons, and private clients recognize the essential, and not previously available, detailed information and illustrations.

The time is now appropriate to separate and simplify— to provide a book that presents the seam method alone and with less instructional text. *Fabulous Fit* is that book.

Experience shows that once an alteration method is understood, most people look to the illustration, not to lengthy text, for instruction and review or reference. *Fabulous Fit* meets this need nicely. Fashion styles most likely to fit without alteration are also identified in *Fabulous Fit*, along with illustrated fashion styles to flatter the figure—to camouflage, draw attention away from, or create illusions that visually balance a particular figure variation. Tips and strategies guaranteed to set the stage for a fabulous fit precede the entire section on individual figure variations

The double page spreads contain a sequence of thought and application the reader can follow and rely on for quick reference in the future. Each spread communicates a lesson and a pattern for practice and comparison. As the user of *Fabulous Fit* studies and practices each "lesson", his or her skill to perceive, interpret and solve the variety of fitting problems will grow. Skill can grow to the point of applying and adapting the seam method of alteration to solve fitting problems anywhere on the figure of men, women and children. The very practical content, coupled with a personable approach, makes *Fabulous Fit* a valuable resource for the pattern maker, home and commercial sewer, clothing teachers and students. It also provides a strong foundation of information essential for image management consultants and clients alike.

1994

Judith Rasband
Orem, Utah

Acknowledgments

The contract for *Fabulous Fit* arrived the day before learning I had breast cancer and would undergo surgery followed by chemotherapy. Faced with uncertain circumstances, I considered not signing the contract. I appreciate the confidence and continued support of my editor, Olga Kontzias, who hesitated not a moment in telling me to, "Sign."

I'd like to thank my reviewers—Leslie Davis Burns, Ellen Goldsberry and Elizabeth Liechty—for their comprehensive remarks and suggestions.

Because people rely on "reading" the pictures, this particular book would be of less value without its many illustrations. I want to express my sincere appreciation to Janet Foutin, who rendered my illustrations by hand and by computer and to Delane Barrus for last-minute computer details. Thanks also to David Jaenisch for perseverance as art director and his professional approach to the design of this book.

Heartfelt thanks go to my family, without whose unfailing love and support this book would not have been completed.

Fabulous Fit

Chapter 1
Fabulous Fit: A Key to Looking Terrific

Fit? You mean fat!" shouted an enthusiastic seminar patron on the subject of proper fit in clothes. And it's true, we often tend to think about clothing fit in terms of extra weight. But fit is a matter of much more than extra weight—and fitting problems, or challenges, are every bit as real for the slim or petite person as for the larger individual.

Fit is a state of mind as well as a state of physical being. The clothes you wear influence the way you think, the way you feel, the way you act, and the way people react or respond to you. When you wear clothes that don't fit, you can't help but think about your body and appearance because you feel physically uncomfortable and unattractive. You act accordingly. You've seen women tugging at a too-tight or too-short skirt and people hitching up too-long or too-loose slacks or skirts. The appearance and the behavior are noticed by others, who respond accordingly.

Positive or Negative Attention?

Wearing clothes that don't fit focuses negative attention on your body—your own attention as well as the attention of others. It's no wonder that even a size 10 woman thinks she's too fat when she's wearing clothing a size too small. If the clothes feel strained or tight, she feels fat! She feels self-conscious, continually aware of tight clothes pressing or rubbing against her body, cutting into her body, and restricting her movement.

Other people also notice poor fit. Garments that pull, gap and ripple or wrinkle are distracting. They draw negative attention to your figure variations and fitting problems. Wearing size 8 when you need size 10 demonstrates insecurity. It declares, "I don't like my body. I'm doing my best to ignore it—or to make you think I'm smaller." And believe me, clothing too small makes you look even larger. If it feels tight, it looks tight. If it looks tight it makes you look even heavier—stuffed in. Tight fitting clothes expose the body and emphasize figure variations you may prefer people didn't notice. They cause you to look out of proportion and out of balance with yourself.

Clothing too large, regardless of style, can also declare dissatisfaction with your body. If overly baggy it just hangs on the body, even on a size 24 figure. It says you have something to hide.

A slightly loose fit—an elegantly loose fit—is the way to look thinner, trimmer, slimmer, smaller. Call it what you like, it works! Dress yourself in clothes that fit, clothes that slip easily over your body with room to move, and you can forget about your body and your size and concentrate on more important matters. You can get on with your life, secure with thoughts and feelings of self-confidence that come from knowing and feeling that your clothes are both comfortable and attractive.

Why Bother with Fabulous Fit?

A fabulous fit eliminates the gaps, ripples or wrinkles that advertise your figure variations and fitting problems. It allows others to focus positive attention on you—your face

"Fit can be more important than style, fabric, color, construction, or price."

JUDITH RASBAND,
CONSELLE INSTITUTE
OF IMAGE MANAGEMENT

and purposeful points of interest. Positive attention goes to design details and coordination, but always comes back to you. One of the easiest and most effective ways to improve or enhance your appearance is to get a fabulous fit in your clothes.

Clothes that fit well:

- Enhance appearance and are attractive.
- Contribute to thoughts and feelings of self-worth, self-esteem, and self-confidence.
- Hang from the shoulders, waist, or hips and fall smoothly over the figure without clinging, binding, pulling, gapping, twisting, or hiking up.
- Enhance the natural relationship between the garmet shape and the shape of your body—design details are in scale and proportion with your body.
- Draw negative attention away from figure variations, conceal and create flattering illusions about those variations.
- Draw positive attention to and emphasize the most attractive areas of the body.
- Adjust naturally to body movement without strain. When not moving, the clothes relax and return to their natural positions, free of stress wrinkles.
- Contribute to an active lifestyle by allowing you to concentrate on more important matters and goals.

Fabulous fit is a must! It's essential to looking your personal or professional best. Plus, you can wear nearly any clothing style attractively if you get it to fit. Clothes that fit require less care and attention. With less strain on them, they look neater, wear better, and last longer.

Fabulous Fit through Knowledge and Experience

The ability to achieve a fabulous fit doesn't come instantly or automatically. It comes with knowledge backed up by experience. Some of that knowledge and experience requires trial and error. You can reduce the error by first learning about the following:

- Your figure and its variations.
- The art of dress.
- Factors that contribute to a fabulous fit.
- Standards to evaluate the fit of your clothes.
- Custom fit and altered clothes.

With knowledge and experience, you'll find you can wear nearly any style you want, as long as it fits right in all the right places. You'll discover that fabric has as much to do with fit as it does with size. You'll realize that even the most perfect color won't make you look beautiful if the clothes don't fit and flatter. I appreciate this little verse, "The bargains I buy may fit my purse, but they don't fit me—and that's their curse." The style may be terrific, the fabric and color gorgeous, the construction high quality, the size you normally wear, and the price exactly right. But if it doesn't fit, it doesn't work.

Chapter 2
Figure Variations

It doesn't take that much "people watching" to discover that figures are different from one another, or to realize that almost nobody has an exactly average, perfect or ideal body. Such bodies simply do not exist. We use the terms to give ourselves a frame of reference for comparison. It helps to know that virtually everybody has some figure variation from the so-called average or ideal. Notice I call them "figure variations," not figure flaws, faults, deformities, liabilities, deviations, inadequacies or abnormalities—all negative terms that assume there is something wrong with us. Such negative words contribute to needless and unhealthy feelings of anxiety and low self-esteem. Be kind to yourself. Figure variation is a descriptive term to use. And remember, everybody has a few figure variations.

Steps to a Fabulous Fit

The first step toward achieving a fabulous fit and looking terrific is to become familiar with your figure and the ways it varies from the average or ideal.

Figures vary from one another in six characteristic ways:

- Height
- Bone size or structure
- Weight
- Proportional body areas
- Contour and figure type
- Posture

These six characteristics are interrelated, each affecting the other. Height, bone size or structure, proportional areas, and the pattern of weight distribution are inherited traits and remain constant throughout your life. Diet, exercise and posture can change weight and specific contours to some extent.

The second step is to accept those variations that you can't change, such as large bones, a proportionally long midriff or large thighs at the side. The third step is to change those variations you can, such as your posture or weight—assuming you will really follow through. Fourth, be grateful you don't have all 85 or more variations. Nobody does. Appreciate the places you do appear more nearly average. And five, regardless of what shape you're in, prepare to present yourself to your best advantage.

Some of the best things clothes can do for you—besides provide warmth, protection and a creative outlet—are to camouflage a figure variation, draw attention away from a variation, or create attractive illusions about a variation. These are the goals of fashion designers, image consultants and smart dressers the world over. They are the essence of sections on *Fashion Styles to Fit and Flatter* in chapter 6. It is the knowledge and ability of individuals to camouflage, direct attention, and create attractive illusions that makes them look so terrific. You can learn to do it, too.

"A fabulous fit begins with a fair assessment of one's body. Starting with accurate body measurements is the key to successful fitting, whether you are buying ready-to-wear, altering garments, or custom fitting patterns."

NAOMI REICH,
UNIVERSITY OF ARIZONA

Height

Height relates directly to bone size and body weight, and together they influence the styles and amounts of clothing you can wear attractively. Three height divisions are usually cited, and they correspond closely to manufacturing measurement standards. They include short or petite, medium or average, and tall. Actual height is measured without shoes, standing on a hard surface floor, not on plush carpet. These divisions can be broken down as follows:

Shorter / Petite	Under 5'4"
Medium / Average	5'4" to 5'7"
Taller	Over 5'7"

Height is a relative characteristic and the above breakdowns are subjective decisions, made as one person is compared to another or to a group of others. Certainly in one social group a woman could be average at 5' 9". In another social group she could be considered tall at 5' 1" if most members of that group are under 4'.

A woman who is 5' 5" is generally considered medium in height but can appear taller when standing next to someone 5' 2", and shorter when standing next to someone 5' 8". That same woman may feel short when trying on clothes in standard sizes that hang too low or long on the figure, but feel taller when trying on petite sized clothes that hit too high or short on the figure.

There are advantages to every height. Shorter women have the advantage of appearing more feminine when they want. They don't have to feel locked out of wearing long or layered looks. The clothes do have to be scaled down so that garment lines lie in proportionally the same places they do on taller women—rather than lower on the figure. Fabric weights often have to be lighter so they don't overwhelm the shorter figure. Taller women have the advantage of strong visual presence and appear to have more authority. The taller figure can carry light- to heavy-weight fabrics and large-scale clothing pieces without looking overwhelmed. More aware of the needs than ever before, manufacturers are making patterns and clothes sized for different heights available through retail and catalog outlets.

Bone Size

Call it bone size, bone structure, or body frame, it refers to the relative size of your bones, measured at the wrist, the elbow or the ankle. These locations are used as reference points because individuals seldom carry extra weight on those areas—at least as compared to the shoulders, hips, etc. The larger your bone size, the more you should expect to weigh, and the more weight you can carry on your bones. Measure around your wrist just in front of the wrist bone (toward your hand) on the area that you use least. From the Conselle Institute, breakdowns in wrist size are listed in Table 2.1, Bone Sizes.

Height	Wrist Measurement	Bone Size/ Frame
Short/Petite (Under 5'4")	5 1/2" or less 5 5/8" to 6" 6 1/8" or more	Small Medium Large
Medium/Average (5'4" to 5'7")	5 3/4" or less 5 7/8" to 6 1/4" 6 3/8" or more	Small Medium Large
Tall (Over 5'7")	6" or less 6 1/8" to 6 1/2" 6 5/8" or more	Small Medium Large

TABLE 2.1
BONE SIZES

At best, these are only guidelines, or averages, intended to give you a starting point for thought and comparison. Regardless of the guideline used, other factors can influence apparent bone size. For example, if the individual is larger in the upper arm, bust and/or hips, the wrist may appear smaller by comparison than the measurement would otherwise indicate.

Bone size is usually consistent throughout the body, but the structural size of proportional areas can vary. For example, the whole upper torso might be structurally small and the structure of the hip or pelvic area be structurally large, or vice versa. This will influence weight distribution and body contours. Regardless of variations in bone structure, you can always select your clothing and alter your patterns to flatter your figure.

Weight

Figures certainly vary in the amount of weight they carry, and weight is a major factor in finding clothes that fit and flatter. However, there's a big difference between skinny and slender, between big and fat, or large and obese. Remember that the ideal figure is culturally defined and changes from place to place and time to time. Cultural ideals range in extremes from skinny to obese.

There is a relatively wide and safe range of ideal weight. Ideal weight refers to that range in which you are likely to live the healthiest and the longest. Many of us might be happier and healthier if we had scales that registered not in pounds or kilograms, but in safe and unsafe zones. Health risks go up on either side. If you are under or over your ideal weight range, you probably know it without a scale. If you look under or overweight, you probably are. The problem here is a matter of objectivity. Not all of us see ourselves as we actually look and the difference can be dangerous.

A height-bone-weight chart can give you a realistic guide for comparison. Some are more accurate than others, but I can't get too excited about a few pounds one way or the other. I've seen so many differing charts, even different versions of supposedly the same Metropolitan Life Insurance Company chart (see Table 2.2). Again, the charts are meant to be only a general guide. Follow the chart across to locate your bone or frame size. Your weight should be somewhere between the ideal weight range given on the chart. If these weights seem a little heavy, realize they are based on a group of women ages 25-59, wearing one inch heels and three pounds of clothing, with muscles in top condition. If younger, subtract one pound for every year under 25. Because firm muscle tissue weighs more, women with less well-toned muscles can lower the range by about five pounds.

Most women want to lose the extra pounds above ideal weight. If you can lose it easily and keep it off, fine. But if you're spending half your life cutting calories to keep off five or ten pounds, it's very difficult to maintain a nutritionally sound diet. Your health risks are greater than the risk of keeping those extra pounds. The fact that a particular weight holds steady is an important sign that you have a set weight level that works for your body. Increased and continued physical exercise is the only way to lower that weight level or "set point" as it is often called. If you are not able to increase the amount of exercise you get, you can still select and alter your clothes to flatter your figure.

Proportional Body Areas

Your figure can be divided into parts, proportions or proportional areas. In general, proportion is defined as the relationship of all parts to one another and of the parts to the whole. For our purposes, proportion refers to the relationship of each part of the body compared to every other part and to the relationship of each part to the total height and mass. Proportion varies greatly among individuals and can be discussed in terms of size, length, width and weight.

You can identify proportional areas of the body by the break points—points where the body silhouette changes in direction, and creates 1) an inward angle at the narrowest point or 2) an outward angle at the widest point. For example, the narrowest curves of the neck and waist angle inward, while the widest curves of the shoulder, bust and hips angle outward. Neck to shoulders is one lengthwise proportional area, bust to waist is another. These areas can be compared to one another, to the entire upper body or to total height.

Break points are often synonymous with joints—shoulder joint, elbow joint, finger joints, hip joint, knee joint, etc. With this in mind, the upper arm from shoulder to elbow can be compared to the lower arm from elbow to wrist, and the entire arm can be compared to the entire upper body or to total height. Using the hip joint as a break point, the upper body or torso can be compared to the lower body or legs.

The supposedly perfect or ideal figure is made up of proportional areas that are harmonious or pleasing to look at in length and width, one compared to another. They are expressed in a ratio of 2:3. That is, the total body height is divided into five equal parts, ideally with 2/5 from head to waist and 3/5 from waist to feet. Proportions for modern fashion figures are usually expressed in a ratio of 3:5, assuming a taller figure that can be divided into eight sections equal in length, with three sections above the waist and five below, allowing more length in the thigh.

Horizontal proportions can also be considered. For example, width across the shoulders is assumed to be the same or slightly wider than width across the hips. Body circumference—measurement around the body—can be compared as well. Like ideal weight range, ideal proportions are subject to cultural and fashion changes. While very few individuals conform to the average or ideal divisions, sizing for patterns and ready-to-wear clothing are based on these divisions.

Height	Small Bone Frame	Medium Bone Frame	Large Bone Frame
4' 10"	102 - 111	109 - 121	118 - 131
4' 11"	103 - 113	111 - 123	120 - 134
5' 0"	104 - 115	113 - 126	122 - 137
5' 1"	106 - 118	115 - 129	125 - 140
5' 2"	108 - 121	118 - 132	128 - 143
5' 3"	111 - 124	121 - 135	131 - 147
5' 4"	114 - 127	124 - 138	134 - 151
5' 5"	117 - 130	127 - 141	137 - 155
5' 6"	120 - 133	130 - 144	140 - 159
5' 7"	123 - 136	133 - 147	143 - 163
5' 8"	126 - 139	136 - 150	146 - 167
5' 9"	129 - 142	139 - 153	149 - 170
5' 10"	132 - 145	142 - 156	152 - 173
5' 11"	135 - 148	145 - 159	155 - 176
6' 0"	138 - 151	148 - 162	158 - 179

TABLE 2.2
HEIGHT AND FRAME SIZES

FIGURE 2.1
EIGHT TYPICAL COMBINATIONS OF FIGURE VARIATIONS.
NOTE WHERE EACH FIGURE IS PROPORTIONALLY NARROWER OR WIDER.

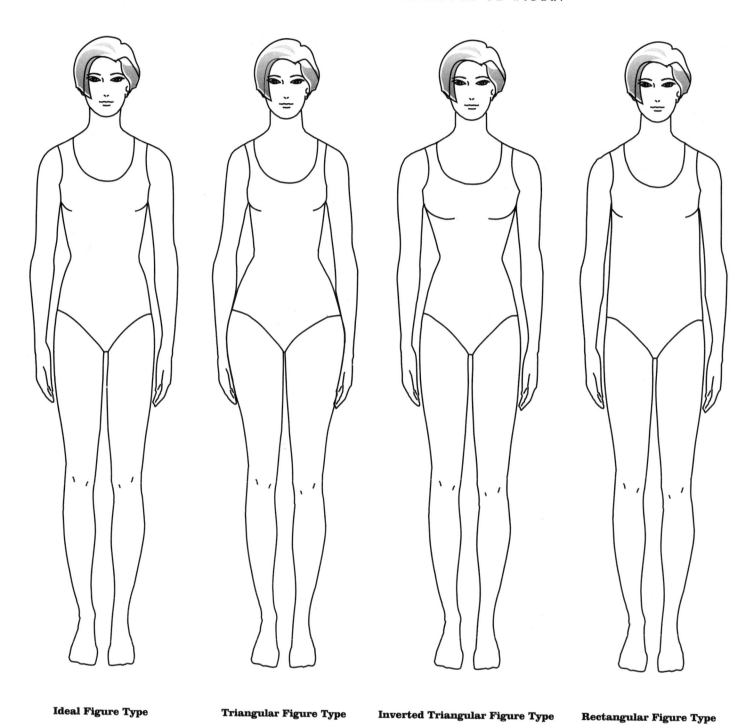

Ideal Figure Type   **Triangular Figure Type**   **Inverted Triangular Figure Type**   **Rectangular Figure Type**

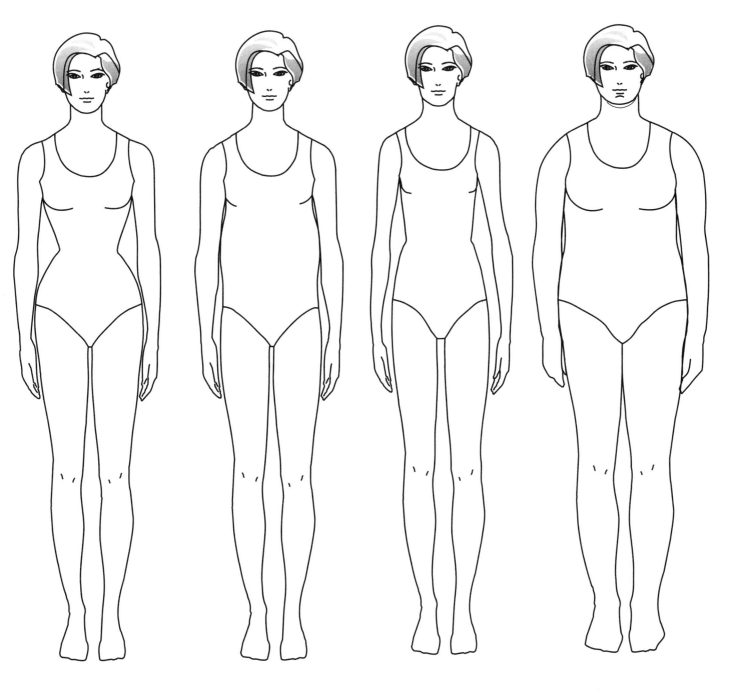

Hourglass Figure Type   **Diamond-shaped Figure Type**   **Tubular Figure Type**   **Rounded Figure Type**

To achieve a balanced, well-proportioned appearance, you need to know how your own body proportions compare to the cultural average or ideal. You need to know where you are proportionally shorter or longer, narrower or wider. Some people have proportionally longer arms and legs with a shorter torso. Many have a proportionally longer midriff and may be average everywhere else, or shorter in the legs (see *illustration 00*). Legs can be average in the thigh area and long in the calf, or vice versa. Shoulders can be proportionally wider than hips or narrower compared to the waist. Some parts of the body can be asymmetrical, that is, not the same on both sides (*see x-ref*). Variations are easy to determine with a tape measure, figure tracing, or photograph. Knowing how you vary from the cultural ideal, you can select clothing styles to lead the eye up or down, in or out, and create the illusion of better balance and proportion.

Contour and Weight Distribution or Figure Type

Contour refers to the curves of your body. Where you curve and how much you curve depends on your bone size and structure, proportional areas, weight, muscle tone, pattern of weight distribution and posture. As discussed earlier, the characteristics affect one another. Everybody's contours vary from a little to a lot. Contours change naturally as we age.

Although we usually think of contours in terms of soft body tissue—fat and muscle—the bones underneath establish the original structure for the curves. Weight determines how much these contours fill out. Diet and exercise affect weight. Exercise can firm up some contours. Undergarments can hold or lift up some of the contours. Posture determines the alignment of body parts and therefore the contours of those parts. Gravity exerts a continual downward pull and by middle age, body tissue begins to droop or sag. What often sags next is your morale. You can't let that happen. Some contours are more fashionable at one time than another. Fashion focused on the bust and buttocks in the Fifties and on shoulders in the Eighties. The bust is back in fashion for the Nineties, so much so that many women are becoming overly concerned about increasing bust size. Tummy tucks, breast reduction, liposuction and other forms of cosmetic surgery may offer solutions for extremely large body contours. If the contours are not so extreme, however, it's well worth knowing how to dress to create the illusion of a more nearly ideal figure and alter clothing when needed.

When it comes to overall body contour, there are several typical patterns of weight distribution. We call them body or figure types. You can recognize or identify them according to the specific areas on the body where weight tends to accumulate, regardless of height. Realize that *not every body conforms exactly to one particular type.* Some women have a variation or two that is atypical. Bone or bust size can be different. Midriff or leg length can be different, and so on. Figure types are simply another guideline to make clothing selection easier, so you're looking for the figure type most similar to yours. In the following set of figure types, all but the ideal are identified in terms of the relative similarity to easily recognized geometric shapes as viewed from the front.

Ideal Figure Type The *ideal* figure used in pattern and clothing design is similar in width in the shoulders and hips, with medium bust, small waist, flat to slightly curved abdomen, moderately curved buttocks and slim thighs. The figure is well balanced with no area exaggerated. There is enough weight to cover the bones and hollows of the body softly and smoothly. (Bust and hip circumference measure the same or similar and waist circumference is about 10 inches smaller.)

Triangular Figure Type This figure appears smaller or narrower above the waist and larger or wider below the waist. Bones are usually small but well-padded below the waist, with weight concentrated in the buttocks, low hips and thighs. The figure appears unbalanced, top to bottom. Shoulders are narrower than hips, or sloped so they appear narrower. The bust is small to medium. The midriff is often longer (not always) with proportionally shorter legs. The waist is small to medium, buttocks are rounded, hips are proportionally wider and rounded, and upper thighs are often heavier. (Dominant low hip or side thigh curve, with a hip circumference that measures 2 inches larger or more than the bust circumference.) Extra weight goes on the lower torso first.

Inverted Triangular Figure Type This figure appears larger or wider above the waist and smaller or narrower below the waist. Bones are usually medium in size and weight is concentrated in the shoulders, upper back and/or bust. The figure appears unbalanced. The shoulder area is comparatively wider than the hip area and/or the bust is medium to large. The midriff is often shorter (not always) and legs may be proportionally longer. The waist is medium to wide. A high hip curve is typical, with lower hips and thighs straighter in line. The buttocks are often flatter. (Dominant high hip curve, with a bust circumference that measures 1 inch larger or more than the hip circumference.) Extra weight goes on the upper torso and high hip area first.

Rectangular Figure Type This figure appears to be nearly the same width at shoulders, waist and hips—nearly straight up and down. The figure is balanced top and bottom, but the waist is not noticeably indented at the sides and appears wide in proportion to the hips. In other words, the midriff and upper hips taper very little toward the waist, if at all. Side thighs are generally the same width as hips. The bust is small to medium. (Waist circumference measures 7 inches or less than bust or hip.) Extra weight gain tends to be fairly evenly distributed over the body.

Hourglass Figure Type This figure appears equally wide and full-rounded in the bust area and hip area, but appears proportionally very small in the waist. The bust is medium to large. The midriff and upper hips taper to a small, well-indented waist. Hips and buttocks are smoothly rounded. The hourglass figure is balanced top and bottom, but is not considered ideal because the very small waist makes the bust and behind appear proportionally larger than they are. (Bust and hip circumference measure the same or similar and waist circumference is 11 inches smaller or more.) Weight gain is fairly evenly distributed above and below the waist. Even with extra weight, the waist remains proportionally smaller.

Two more figures remain to be discussed. They may or may not be considered specific types, depending on your point of view. However, they are typical, easily recognized, and qualify for specific clothing selection and alteration advice.

Diamond-shaped Figure Type This figure is typified by comparatively narrow shoulders and hips in combination with a wide midriff and waist. The midriff and upper hips do not taper inward toward the waist, but appear to expand outward at the waist. The bust is often small, with a high hip curve and straight or inwardly tapered side thighs. The buttocks are often smaller and legs are proportionally thinner. Weight is concentrated in the midriff, waist and abdomen area and extra weight goes on there first. (Mid-body circumference measures larger than bust or hip circumference.)

Tubular Figure Type This figure is similar to the rectangular figure, only thinner because weight is considerably below the average range. This figure appears straight up and down—with comparatively narrow shoulders and hips, small bust, waist and buttocks, thin arms and legs—simply because there is very little flesh to distribute over the bones of the body. With weight gain to within the average range, this figure will appear more like one of the figure types mentioned above.

Rounded Figure Type A truly rounded figure is so-called because body areas are full-rounded all over. Weight is noticeably above the average range. Typically, the upper back and upper arms are larger and rounding. The bust, midriff, waist, abdomen, buttocks, hips and upper legs are larger and rounding. With weight reduction into the average range, this figure will appear more like one of the above figure types.

Knowing your general figure type makes clothing selection easier. Women with the same general figure type, regardless of height and size, are most easily flattered by the same or similar set of clothing styles. In other words, all triangular, all rectangular, all diamond...and so on, are most easily flattered by a particular set of clothing styles designed in such a way to counterbalance their particular figure type.

Furthermore, and for example, if a triangular-figured individual loses weight, she does not automatically qualify for clothes that can be worn by someone with a nearly ideal figure. Unless weight change is extreme, leading to a rounded or tubular figure, characteristic bone structure and pattern of weight distribution remain the same. Granted, becoming smaller in the hip/thigh area will expand her options, but she is still most easily fitted and flattered by styles that counterbalance the triangular-shaped figure. It is important to note, however, that clothing styles you might think would be unflattering for a certain figure type often become flattering when custom-fitted to the individual figure and combined with appropriate accessories, particularly shoes.

Recognizing your body's overall contours and figure type will make it easier to understand how your body relates to the average/ideal figures used in pattern and clothing design, and manufacture. It will give you an objective guide for selecting clothing styles that make visual sense and flatter your figure. It will also alert you to clothing areas that may need to be altered.

Posture

You may not have thought about it, but poor posture is perhaps the most common figure variation. Posture reflects how you think and feel about yourself. Overly erect posture may communicate an air of arrogance, while slumped posture tends to say you feel tired, ill, unattractive, unimportant, or that you're uninterested in life. Fatigue, weak muscles and extra weight can certainly contribute to poor posture as well as ill-fitting or high-heeled shoes, a lumpy or saggy mattress, poorly-designed chairs and sofas, sleeping with your head on a pile of pillows, carrying a heavy bag, books or a baby on one side and bending over a desk for long periods of time. Even poor eyesight can create that "hang-dog" look as the head is thrust forward in an attempt to see more clearly. Typical examples of poor posture are illustrated for comparison to your own posture.

To further evaluate your own posture, hang a weighted string from the top of a mirror. The edge of a door will also work. Turn sideways to the string or door edge and assume a relaxed but normal stance, with your weight evenly distributed over both feet. Don't attempt to correct your posture at this point. The string or door should line up with the middle of your ear lobe, neck, shoulder and arm at the elbow, pass just to the back of your wrist, line up with the middle of your hip joint and knee, then pass slightly in front of the center of your ankle.

If you prefer, you can check your posture by standing up next to a wall, with your heels about an inch away from the wall. Good posture is evident if the back or your head, shoulders, shoulder blades and buttocks touch the wall. You should be able to insert your hand in the space between the wall and the small of your back at the waist.

Correct posture assumes a balanced alignment of your body parts over one another.

• Your head and neck should be centered over your shoulders with your chin level or parallel to the floor. You don't want the double chin that results when you tuck it in or down, nor do you want to thrust your head too far forward.

• Your chest should be lifted slightly, but without arching your back.

FIGURE 2.2
GEOMETRIC SHAPES FUNCTION AS VISUAL CUES TO NOTE WHERE THE FIGURE IS
PROPORTIONALLY NARROWER OR WIDER, AND TO IDENTIFY THE GENERAL FIGURE TYPE.

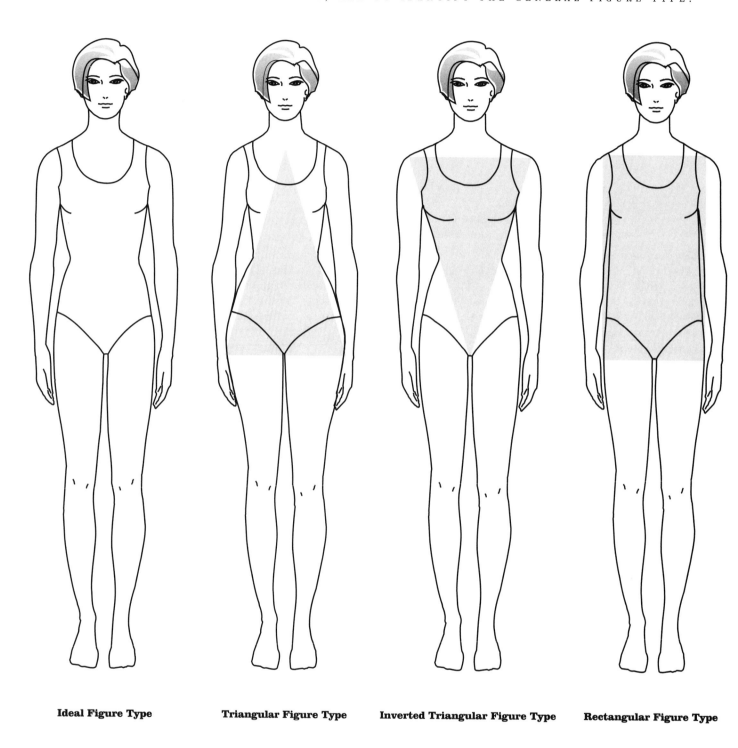

Ideal Figure Type   **Triangular Figure Type**   **Inverted Triangular Figure Type**   **Rectangular Figure Type**

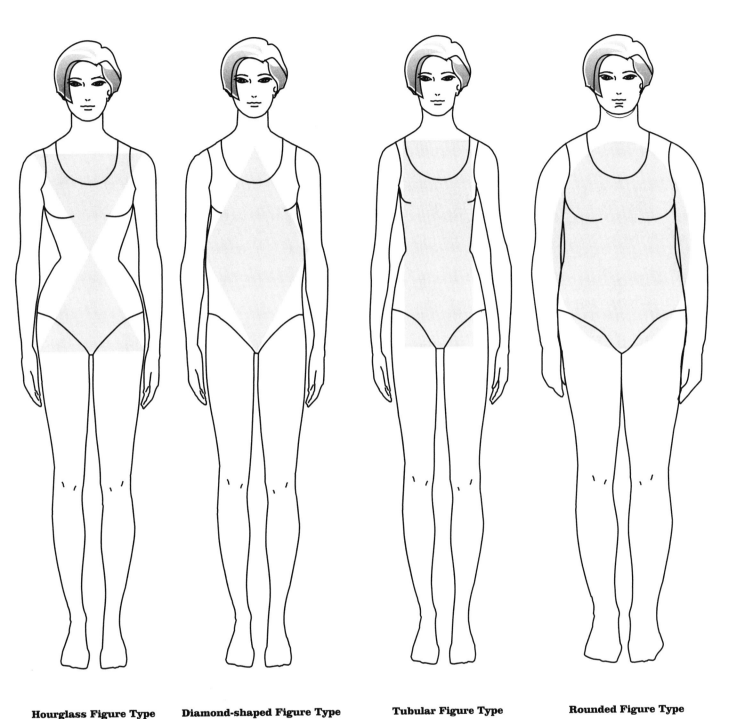

Hourglass Figure Type   **Diamond-shaped Figure Type**   **Tubular Figure Type**   **Rounded Figure Type**

- With your back straight, your shoulders should be squarely set, but relaxed. Don't squeeze your shoulder blades together. That's strictly for West Point.

- Pull in or tighten your abdominal muscles. Notice I said "pull" the muscles in, not "suck" them in. You don't have to hold your breath. Let your muscles do the work.

- Your hips should be level, not tilted forwards or back. Tighten and tuck your seat "under." Don't let it "sway" back or forward.

- Let your arms hang relaxed at your sides, with your elbows bent slightly forward.

- Your knees should be straight but not stiff, relaxed but not bent.

- With your feet slightly apart and toes pointing straight ahead, rock back and forth just a little until you can feel that your body weight is balanced evenly between the heels and balls of your feet.

Don't be discouraged if you discover your posture is less than perfect. You can improve or correct it if you commit yourself to regular practice and retrain your body parts to assume their proper position. If you've slumped around for years, it may feel awkward at first and will take a little time. Stand next to a wall and assume a "corrected" posture. Then walk away from the wall and hold this posture for a minute. Think about how it feels. Check yourself against the wall periodically as you practice. Keep a mental picture of how good posture looks and feels as you stand, walk and sit.

Proper diet and exercise may produce the figure you want, but if you do not carry it correctly, your figure will never look terrific. Even an ideal figure can appear unbalanced and out of proportion if posture is poor. Slumped, slouched, rounded and swayed posture causes shoulders to slope, breasts to sag, stomach and buttocks to protrude. Poor health and a host of fitting problems follow. Conversely, a less than ideal figure can appear more nearly ideal by standing and sitting correctly. Fitting problems can often be eliminated or greatly improved if you simply stand up straight. It's worth the effort to work on your posture.

Chapter 3
Set Yourself Up for a Fabulous Fit

With an accurate mental image of your figure in mind and your posture up to par, you're ready to consider specific factors that influence the fit of your clothes. Before getting into the stores to shop, pay attention to the undergarments and shoes you wear or take shopping.

Undergarments

Wear well-fitted undergarments, ideally the pieces you expect to wear with the clothes you try on. Certain clothing styles demand specific underwear appropriate for just that style—straight or flared slip, half or full slip, strapless or long-line bra, camisole, control-top pantyhose, etc.

Make sure the undergarment itself fits properly. Think of what goes on under your clothes as your personal support system. It will affect the look, the feel, and the fit of what goes over. Even the finest clothes fit poorly and look out of shape—or make you look out of shape—if you wear them over undergarments that don't fit. Well-fitted undergarments can comfortably lift, support and control sagging body areas, eliminate the apparent figure variation, and improve the fit of your clothes.

If you are not sure your undergarments fit as well as they should, take time to shop for the right styles and sizes for your figure. Sales personnel in many lingerie departments and specialty stores are trained to help you get a proper fit. (See *Table 3.1, Tips for Fitting and Buying Undergarments.*)

Shoes

Wear, or take with you, the shoes (or a similar pair) that you plan to wear with the outfit you try on. Shoe style and heel height influence the fit, hang, and attractiveness of the clothes you wear. Very often an inch or two of heel height is just what's needed to visually lengthen your leg for better proportion and overall balance. A tapered wedge can often give you the height you need along with the comfort of a flat. Heavy, chunky or bulky shoes seldom flatter a skirted leg. T-strap shoes are for slim legs and ankles only.

If you wear high heels, 2½ to 3 inches or more, make sure they don't distort your posture and therefore the fit of your clothes. Many women wearing higher heels arch their back unnaturally to maintain their balance. If you're unable to stand straight in high heels, choose a lower mid-height heel instead. If you're going to shop for dress clothes, I suggest you also wear or take along a pair of pantyhose to try with your shoes. Socks or knee-hi's can spoil the look of a short dress. (See *Table 3.2, Tips for Fitting and Buying Shoes.*)

Sizes Differ with Stores, Brands, and Designers

The U.S. Department of Commerce determined standard measurements for each size, based on average body measurements. Although there is general industry cooperation, clothing designers and manufacturers have their own reasons for changing the standards to meet the needs of their perceived market. Those reasons include differing ideas on how clothes

> ## *"Any figure type can wear any style…as long as it fits properly."*
>
> PATI PALMER,
> PALMER/PLETCH ASSOCIATES

should be cut, how much ease to allow, and ways to cut costs. Some of their reasons are based on the way you are shaped. Others are based on the way the designer is shaped. Designers often change their standard model along with changes in the average American figure, their own or their target customer. American designers and manufacturers of more expensive clothing go the extra inch to flatter the ego with generously cut sizes, the idea being that women will pay more for a size 8 than they will for size 12.

It's the same story with brands. Each brand is sized according to a different model, with more expensive brands allowing a more generous cut of fabric, and less expensive brands cut skimpy to save money. If a manufacturer cuts hundreds of size 10 dresses just a little bit smaller, it can save hundreds of dollars in fabric and sell each dress at a lower price. So, in more expensive or designer clothes you may fit into a size or two smaller and in less expensive garments you may have to move up the rack. Foreign import brands are sized differently still, with European and Oriental sizes often cut smaller than American sizes.

To complicate what is already complex, types of garments are not sized alike. Blouses and shirts are sized differently than sweaters, dresses differently than coats, pants differently than pant suits and still differently from skirted suits. Garment style makes another difference. Wide leg pants and flared or full skirts often let you drop down a size while fitted pants and skirts make you move up a size or two. And finally, be aware that fabric makes another difference. Fluffy, thick or bulky fabric takes up space and makes for a tighter fit. You may need a larger size for a comfortable and flattering fit.

This all adds up to frustration when shopping for ready-to-wear clothes and a smorgasbord of sizes in your closet. Don't limit yourself to one size or category of sizes. Clothes within a store are generally grouped together in categories, according to the figure they are designed to fit. American sizing categories typically include Juniors, Teens, Misses, Women's, Half-sizes, and possibly Petite, Tall and Queen or other similarly descriptive terms. If you're not sure which category fits you best, try styles you like from among any group. (See *Table 3.3, Tips for Fitting and Buying Clothes that Fit.*)

Styles to Suit Your Figure Type

Within a size range, shop for patterns and clothes in styles that make visual sense for your figure or figure type—styles you can expect to accommodate, balance and flatter your figure. Line and shape are the elements of design that combine to create the style of a garment. Unless you have an ideal figure type, clothing styles need enough ease to allow the fabric to flow smoothly over proportionally larger areas of your figure, and extra fullness or fabric to fill out proportionally smaller areas. You are looking for a logical, natural, and aesthetic relationship between the shape of your body and the shape of the garment—between the body silhouette and garment silhouette. In all cases, either the body shape or the garment shape will be dominant—one or the other. It is smart to choose a dominant garment shape and allow your body shape to be subordinate.

SET YOURSELF UP FOR A FABULOUS FIT **19**

TABLE 3.1
TIPS FOR FITTING AND BUYING
UNDERGARMENTS

Ease

Ease is the difference between the actual measured size of the body and the measured size of the garment, as intended by the designer. The amount of ease required for comfort, movement, and an attractive appearance depends on the clothing design, the fabric, the figure, the occasion where the clothing will be worn and, of course, personal preference. Some people simply prefer more room in their clothes. The trend in oversized clothing during the Eighties has led me to want extra ease in my own clothes.

Wearing Ease Every garment must have enough ease to move comfortably. This is called wearing ease. Wearing ease can range from 2 to 4 inches at the chest to allow for moving and breathing; 1 to 1½ inches at the waistline to allow for bending over or raising the arms; and 2 to 4 inches at the hips to allow for sitting, walking, etc. These are the minimum amounts of fabric you should be able to pinch out at the side of a garment when you try it on. These amounts are especially important the more fitted the garment is.

Fashion trends can bring about changes in generally accepted amounts of wearing ease. Regardless of fashion trends, however, clothing is designed to fit and hang from the top. Jackets, coats, dresses, shirts, sweaters, and vests are designed to fit and hang smoothly from the shoulders. Skirts and slacks are designed to fit and hang smoothly from the waist or upper hips. If there is not enough ease, clothing strains, pulls and binds uncomfortably against the body, emphasizing body contours and figure variations. This means you need a larger size or a looser, fuller style—and that leads to design ease.

Design Ease The degree of closeness, looseness, or fullness of fit necessary for the style, or silhouette, is called design ease. Some clothes are designed to be very closely fitted and others are intended to be slightly fitted. A very close-fitting garment may include less than minimum wearing ease. Other clothes are designed to fit slightly loose and still others are intended to hang very loose or full on the body. They include more than minimum amounts of wearing ease. Fullness beyond wearing ease is created by adding flare, flared insets, gathers, shirring, tucks, or pleats. Many interesting and attractive clothing designs include a combination of close and loose or full fit. They work wonders to camouflage, balance and flatter a variety of figure variations.

Reinforcing and Countering

Reinforcing and countering are the two most effective ways to control the way your figure appears in clothes—to help you decide if the clothes make visual sense for your figure.

Reinforcing/Repetition

You can use all the elements of design—line, shape, color, texture, and pattern to repeat and therefore strengthen or emphasize a particular figure trait or area. When shopping for patterns and clothes in styles that make visual sense for your figure or figure type, you want to select garments that reinforce only the areas of your figure you consider most attractive. You don't want to select a garment that reinforces and therefore exposes or emphasizes a figure variation that you don't want to draw attention to.

For example, if you have a noticeably large abdomen you do not want to expose or emphasize, it doesn't make sense to shop for a pattern or an outfit with a close-fitting midriff and skirt. The close fit will repeat the outline of those body areas—expose and emphasize the size of your abdominal. Reinforcing goes beyond the elements of line and shape to include fabric and color. A heavy knit fabric will add even more to the visual size and weight of the abdominal area. A bright color in shiny fabric will attract attention and visually enlarge the area. You're smart to select an outfit that provides some contrast or countering effect to camouflage and create the illusion of a flatter abdomen.

Countering/Contrast

You can use all the elements of design—line, shape, color, texture, and pattern—to counteract and therefore neutralize or minimize a figure trait or area. In selecting clothing styles that make visual sense for your figure or figure type, you want to select a garment that counters a figure variation you consider unattractive. When countering, some feature of the garment design covers, conceals or camouflages the figure variation, leads attention away from the variation, and creates an attractive illusion about the variation.

For example, if you have a noticeably large abdomen and don't want to reinforce or draw attention to it, you're smart to select a loose-fitting skirt that flows easily over the abdomen, and a top with some fullness above the waist to make the abdomen below look flatter. If there is some flare in the skirt, chances are no one will notice your abdomen at all. The garment shape or silhouette is dominant and counters or takes attention away from your abdomen.

Countering also works to create the illusion of better vertical balance and proportion. In the case of proportionally shorter chest, midriff, lower torso or legs, the idea is to draw attention in the direction that will visually lengthen those areas, and vice versa if the need is to visually shorten those areas.

It helps to think of reinforcing in terms of repetition or sameness—it's the same line type, line direction, and the same shape. Think of countering in terms of contrast or opposites—it means opposite line type, line direction, and shape. Because the eye follows body and style lines, attention-getting lines should be used in the location and direction you want to emphasize, not in the location or direction you

Tips for Fitting and Buying Shoes

- If new shoes are needed, shop for them later in the day. Your feet swell during the course of the day. To insure a comfortable fit, you need to buy new shoes when your feet are at their largest, not their smallest.
- When buying shoes, have both feet measured. Almost no one has both feet exactly the same size. Buy to fit the larger foot and request an innersole pad to improve the fit on the smaller foot.
- Buy shoes that fit, regardless of size. Standard sizes vary among manufacturers. Size 8B from one company may fit differently than size 8B from another company. There is no way you can stand or walk "tall" in shoes too tight and you'll only slop around in shoes too large.
- Shoes should fit about one-half inch longer than your longest toe. Press your thumb down on the tip of the shoe and wiggle your toes to check the toe space.
- The sides of the shoe should fit smoothly against the sides of your feet, with the widest part of the shoe positioned at the widest part of your foot—across the ball or joint area of your foot. If shoes gap at the sides as you walk, the shoes are too wide. The arch of the shoe should provide comfortable support, not pressure, under your own arch.
- Shoes should fit comfortably snug around your heel. To test, raise up slightly on tiptoe. The heel should stay in place, not slide up and down or off. Your foot should not slide forward.

TABLE 3.2
TIPS FOR FITTING AND BUYING SHOES

T A B L E   3 . 3
T I P S   F O R   B U Y I N G   C L O T H E S   T H A T   F I T

want to minimize. If you have a figure trait you want to emphasize, fine. Reinforce the line or shape of the figure with the same clothing line or shape. If it's not a trait you want to expose or emphasize, then counter it with lines and shapes of the opposite type or in the opposite direction.

For example, a round neckline repeats a rounded face, and puff or melon sleeves repeat the shape and size of large arms. Thick, bulky, heavy fabric will reinforce the effect. On the other hand, an angular notched collar counters a round face or round shoulders. Moderate shoulder pads further serve to counter the look of round shoulders. A full-rounded figure will be flattered by straight lines and angles that counter the roundness of the figure and lead to the face. Light to medium weight fabric, flat or non-bulky, in a cool, darker, or muted color will increase the countering effect.

As another example, a thin, bony figure has relatively straight body lines and angles. It needs to be attractively softened and filled out with slightly curved, loose-fitting clothing lines to counter the narrowness, straight lines and angles of the body. Don't go to extreme, however, or you will lose the effectiveness of this technique. Too much contrast magnifies the difference in size. Thin legs, for example, will appear even thinner under a crisp or stiff, wide, full-rounded bouffant skirt. A skirt with soft or moderate fullness is what's needed. Color is an element of design that can be used to reinforce or counter the look of your figure or a figure variation. Warm, light or bright colors cause the figure or body area to appear slightly larger and heavier. Cool, dark, dull or muted colors cause the figure or body area to appear slightly smaller and less weighty. Notice I said "slightly." It is not a great enough difference to limit anyone from wearing a wide range of colors. If the clothes fit and flatter—with enough ease—larger women can wear red and white and look absolutely beautiful.

Clothing styles that make visual sense for typical figure types depend on countering techniques. They allow enough ease and/or fullness to accommodate the body shape, camouflage predictable figure variations, balance the figure, and create the illusion of more perfect proportions. Working with the elements of line and shape, it is easy to diagram and discuss what is needed for any figure type or variation.

Triangular Figure Type The most flattering styles for this figure feature width or fullness above the waist—in the shoulders, sleeves or bodice—to balance body width or weight below the waist and create the illusion of better proportions. At the same time, the skirt or pants must be loose-fitting to flow easily over and camouflage the lower torso—abdomen, hip, thigh, and buttocks. Ideally, style lines or details in the outfit draw attention away from the lower torso.

Extended shoulders, shoulder pads, fuller sleeves, wide necklines, open collars, shoulder yokes and tops bloused at the waist fill out the upper torso. A-line, flared and straight-hanging dirndl or pleated skirts are styled to flow easily over the lower torso. Center front vertical lines and closures draw attention inward, then up and down for a slimming effect. Neckline detail draws attention upward toward the face. Hemline detail draws attention down. All draw attention away from width or weight in the lower torso.

Inverted Triangular Figure Type The most flattering styles for this figure feature soft fullness below waist—in skirts or slacks—to balance body width or weight above the waist and create the illusion of better proportions. At the same time, tops must be loose-fitting to flow easily over and camouflage the upper torso—shoulders, bust, back and midriff. Ideally, style lines or details in the outfit draw attention inward or down and away from the widest or largest areas in the upper torso.

Take advantage of fullness in the way of flares, gathers or pleats in skirts and pants. That doesn't mean going to the extreme of bubble and bouffant shapes. It also doesn't eliminate shoulder pads. Broad shoulders can be a fashion asset. In addition, shoulder pads can lift fabric to fit more smoothly over a larger bust. Again, just don't go to extreme.

Rectangular Figure Type Flatter this figure with clothing styles that are very loose-fitting or partially fitted to flow easily over the midriff, waist and abdomen. Create the illusion of an indented waist with loose fit above the waist, or above and below the waist, and by drawing attention into the center of the body at the waist.

Overblouses and tunic tops, tops bloused at the waist, shift, chemise and shirtwaist dresses are obvious styles to consider. Layered outfits work wonders to camouflage the silhouette. Jackets, sweaters and vests worn open in front draw attention inward and create a slimming vertical line. A belt worn under creates the look of a waist. Select belts with center front detail, then wear them slightly loose. Look for design lines and details in the neckline that draw attention upward to the face, and details in the hem if legs look great.

Hourglass Figure Type Enhance this figure by visually reducing the difference between full-rounded bust and hip curves and a very small waist. Do this with loose fit in the bust and hip area, and by filling out the mid-body area, just slightly.

A cinch belt is the last thing this figure needs. When you emphasize or draw attention to a very small waist, you only emphasize the larger bust and hip area by extreme contrast—making them appear even larger than they are. Counter this effect with ease above and below the waist and a slightly loose fit at the waist. A slightly bloused bodice may be all you need.

Diamond-shaped Figure Type This figure demands clothing styles that feature width or fullness above and below the waist, to balance width or weight in the mid-body area and create the illusion of wider shoulders and hips. At the same time, styles must be very loose-fitting to camouflage and flow easily over the midriff, waist and abdomen. Ideally, style lines or details in the outfit draw attention away from the middle of the body, or skillfully create the illusion of a waistline in much the same way as with a rectangular figure type.

Clothing can extend the shoulder line and fall straight down to cover and camouflage the entire torso. Longer shirts, overblouses and jackets, flared, tent and caftan dresses provide an easy fit. Include design lines or details that lead attention into the center at the waist and up to the face. Light to medium weight layered looks are recommended.

Long over short and loose over slim are looks you can depend on. Well-tailored, straight leg slacks look terrific. Don't try to cinch in the waist. You'll look stuffed in and feel miserable.

Rounded Figure Type Flatter this figure with straight lines and angles that counter the soft roundness of the figure, and with lines that draw attention to the face. A comfortably loose-fitting belt, wit or without a contrasting buckle, effectively draws attention inward at the waist. A loose-fitting, second layer jacket or tunic worn open up the front, in a color that contrast with the color of the layer beneath, creates a very noticeable vertical line. This line draws attention inward and up the center front for a slimming visual effect.

A round neckline or yokeline repeats and emphasizes a rounded face. Puff or melon sleeves repeat the shape and size of large upper arms. If this is not the effect you want, don't choose them. Thick, heavy fabric reinforces the effect, exactly what you may not want to do. On the other hand, a notched collar effectively counters a round face or round shoulders. Moderately sized shoulder pads further serve to counter the look of round shoulders and upper arms. Light to medium wight fabric, flat or non-bulky, in a cool, dark or muted color and increase the countering effect and visual slim the figure.

Tubular Figure Type Clothing designed with slightly curved, loose-fitting lines will counter the narrowness and bony angels of a thin figure. Don't go to extreme, however, or you will lose the effectiveness of this technique. Too much contrast magnifies the difference in size and shape. Thin legs will appear even thinner under a crisp or stiff, wide, full-rounded bouffant skirt.

A skirt with soft or moderate fullness is what's needed. Angular style lines in the neck and bodice can be effectively layered to fill out the figure. Angular pleat lines in skirts and pants add silhouette of the figure. Medium and moderately heavy fabric with some bulk are among the options for thin figures. Again, don't go to extreme. Extremely heavy or bulky fabric can overpower a thin figure.

If you're getting the impression that a slightly bloused top is flattering to all figure types, you're right. Design lines and details that draw attention up toward the face also work for all figure types.

A traditional convertible collar is the most classic and flattering collar style, precisely because it combines interesting lines and shape to frame the face and pull attention up to it. Epaulets on the shoulders have the same effect. Topstitching, piping and contrasting colors in the area reinforce the effect.

Color is an element of design that can be used to reinforce or counter the look of your figure or a figure variation. Warm, light or bright colors cause the figure or body area to appear only slightly larger and heavier. Cool, dark, dull or muted colors cause the figure or body area to appear slightly smaller and less weighty. Notice I said "slightly." It is not a great enough difference to limit anyone from wearing a wide range of colors. If the clothes fit and flatter — with enough ease — larger women can wear red and white and look absolutely beautiful.

If you're not sure how a style might fit or relate to your figure, then by all means, try it on. It may look terrible, but then again, it may look terrific.

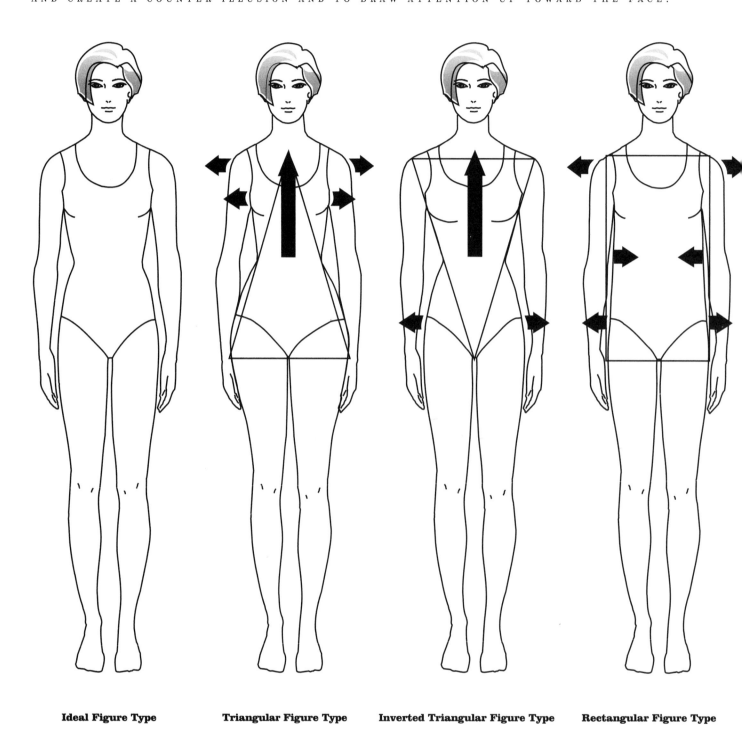

Ideal Figure Type   **Triangular Figure Type**   **Inverted Triangular Figure Type**   **Rectangular Figure Type**

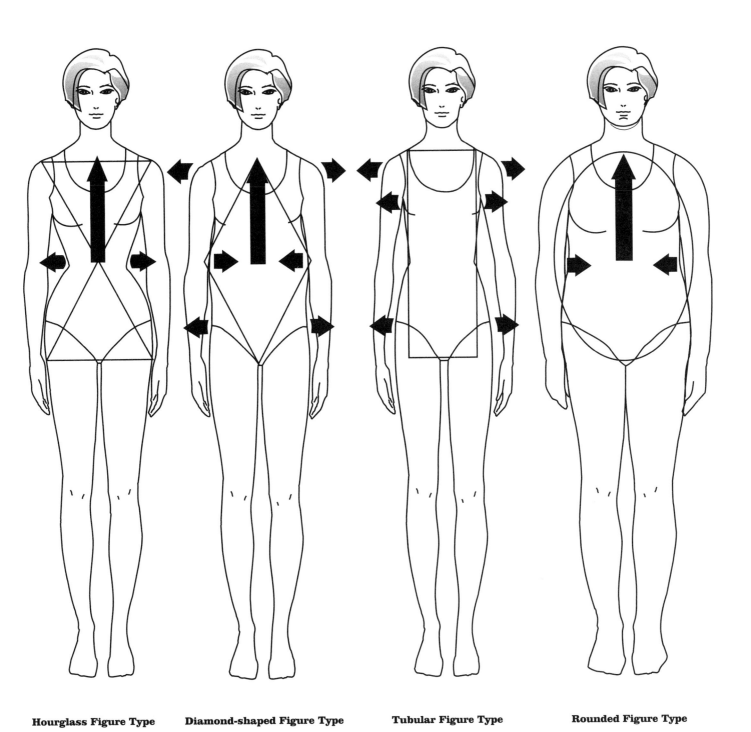

Hourglass Figure Type   **Diamond-shaped Figure Type**   **Tubular Figure Type**   **Rounded Figure Type**

Passing a rack of cotton-knit summer dresses on sale, I asked the clerk why they were so drastically reduced in price, and so soon in the season. The loose-fitting style was bound to be cool and comfortable in mid-summer heat. "We couldn't get anyone to try them on," she said with a shrug. "You must admit, they're pretty plain and shapeless hanging on the rack."

You can't always tell how great a dress will look until you get it off the hanger and onto you. Many fabrics are designed to drape beautifully on the figure. All they really need are hips and shoulders to give them shape. At the same time, remain open to new looks or new lengths and think how you might adapt them to work for you.

Quality

As you find styles in sizes you want to try on, examine the quality. Shop for the best quality you can afford—quality in fabric, cut, and construction. Poor quality fabric won't hang or drape well and may be cut off grain, setting the stage for poor fit before it's even stitched.

Fabric
Don't assume that fabric from 100 percent natural fiber—cotton, linen, silk, and wool—is better than a partial percent. Every fiber and fabric, natural, synthetic or blended, is available in several levels of quality from low to high. Good quality fabric feels good, not flimsy, scratchy or brittle. It is free of flaws and the weave holds together. Tailored-style clothing requires fabric firm enough to support the shape of the garment without revealing yours. Softly-styled clothing requires fabric pliable enough to drape, gather or flare appropriately over your body.

Grainline
Simply stated, grainline refers to the direction and position of the yarns in woven cloth and the loops in knitted fabric. Along the lengthwise grain, yarns run parallel to the finished selvage edge of the fabric. Yarns are perpendicular to the floor at center front and center back. Along the crosswise grain, yarns lie between, or at right angles to the selvages. Yarns are parallel to the floor across the chest, upper back and hip. Bias grain runs diagonally across the lengthwise and crosswise yarns.

Grain controls the way the fabric hangs or drapes on the body—outer fashion fabric as well as support fabric and lining inside. When the lengthwise and crosswise yarns lie on grain, at right angles to each other, the garment hangs evenly on both sides of the body. Balanced grain makes a balanced garment. A garment or sections of a garment can also be cut on the bias grain, diagonally across the straight grain. They hang evenly when cut correctly.

A garment that looks pulled, puckered, twisted, saggy or baggy has likely been cut or stitched off grain—against the natural position of the yarns. The grain is out of line. Stripes and plaids woven into the fabric will bow or sag, compounding the problem. Do not buy a garment that is unbalanced. The garment will hang crooked and never fit well. All the pressing in the world won't help and the problem will probably get worse with washing.

If grainlines are correctly balanced but the garment does not fit the figure, grainlines will slope or bow out of line as it is pulled toward the larger area of the figure needing more fabric. Altering to correct the fit will usually allow fabric grainlines to resume their natural positions.

Cut
Better quality clothing is often cut better, with wider seam and hem allowances to alter as needed. Patterns such as stripes, plaids and prints, are well-placed on the body and matched where possible. Unmatched patterns draw attention to those areas of the body where they lie. A poorly placed pattern can emphasize a body area or figure variation you'd just as soon minimize.

Construction
Poor quality construction leads to poor fit. Seams or darts that pucker or twist because of the way they've been sewn draw attention to themselves and to the area of the body where they lie. You are looking for smooth, secure, finished seams and darts. You need gathers, pleats, tucks, vents, and slits that hang straight and smooth, without excess bulk. Collars, lapels and cuffs should lie smooth and flat as designed. You don't need a bulky collar that pokes out or lapels that bubble and ripple across your chest. Plackets, casings, waistbands, zippers and button openings should also lie flat and smooth without bubbles or bulk. Pockets, belts and trim should be well placed, in scale with the garment and your body. They should never draw attention to places where you don't want attention to go.

Pressing
Poor quality pressing can ruin the fit of the finest clothes. Depending on the fiber and fabric, incorrect pressing can shrink, stretch and crease areas meant to be flat or flatten areas meant to be shaped. A well-pressed garment maintains the original shape and is free of wrinkles, folds, bubbles, puckers or pleats not intended in the design.

You may have to spend more on better quality clothes to get the fit you want, but they don't have to be top of the line or top dollar. Discount and sale prices can keep costs within reason. Be prepared to spend the most money to get great fit on items you wear most often and on important occasions. You can often afford to pay less and get less if the item is for short term or casual at-home wear. If you have difficulty in getting tops to fit, buy better tops, then spend less for what goes on the bottom, and vice versa. Even among several of the same item on the rack, there can be differences in quality. It pays to compare and buy only the best at the price you can afford.

The Dressing Room

When you've found one or more items you want to try on, double check the color, the quality and the care it requires. As you walk around the department or store, carry the piece or pieces of clothing you want to try on and look for garments that will coordinate. Make sure it fits your lifestyle, your personal style, your budget and your existing wardrobe. Then head for the fitting or dressing rooms. Choose the largest one you can find, preferably a private one. Examine the fit of the clothes in front of a full-length mirror—ideally a three-way full-length mirror or two mirrors set at appropriate angles. Accept assistance from the sales clerk only when you're ready to try on the garments you've selected. Don't be intimidated by offers for assistance. Simply say, "I'm still looking, thank you," or "I'll let you know when I'm ready." This goes double in the dressing room. Don't be pressured into making a decision. You've got lots of things to look at and consider before you decide to buy or not to buy.

- Move around. See how the clothes look in action—front, back and sideways. Bend over, squat down, sit down, get up and walk around. Reach out, raise your arms as though combing your hair. Stretch a little. Swing your arms gently back and forth. If you are trying on active sportswear, go through the appropriate motions.

- Close your eyes and concentrate on comfort. It's not enough to look good. The clothes must feel good. Do they feel tight anywhere? If so, open your eyes and focus on that area. Do the clothes lie smooth or do they twist and pull under strain? Do they wrinkle or hang to one side?

- Start at the top of the garment and work down to check the fit. Check the neck and collar. This part is close to the face, and eye level, so it is readily noticed. It is also the most difficult and expensive area to alter. Check the shoulders, upper back, chest, bust and sleeve. Continue down the body, looking at darts, seamlines, grainline, closures, design details, waistline, and hemline.

- Walk out into the corridor or main selling area and stand 8 to 10 feet away from a mirror for a full-length view with better perspective. Distance does wonders to give you a realistic view of what others will see. Dressing rooms are notorious for lights too dim or too bright and mirrors that reflect what you don't want to see. Often, if you look good in the clothes in the dressing room, you can bet you'll look terrific out in the real world. Make sure you look the way you want to be seen.

When you find what fits, and depending on the item, consider buying in multiples. Slacks for example, are not easy to fit. When you find a pair you like that fits, buy them in more than one color. The cost at the moment will be outweighed by the convenience of not having to repeat the same search for a long time.

Save the tag from clothing brands or designers that fit you particularly well. Write the name of the store or catalog company you bought it from to simplify the search next time around.

Clothing Care

The fit and appearance of your clothes depends on how you handle and hang or fold your clothes each day. It depends on how you clean and press your clothes as well as how often.
Practice the following points:

- Change out of your more expensive, quality, or delicate clothes to less expensive, durable clothes for relaxing, housework, homework, or yardwork.

- Handle your clothes gently. Dress and undress carefully to avoid stretching, as well as snags, rips and tears.

- Remove items from pockets so they won't sag and bulge out of shape.

- Remove belts from belt loops and hang separately.

- Always hang up your clothes immediately after you take them off. Well, almost always and almost immediately. Letting clothes pile up on the furniture or floor puts in the wrinkles and ruins the shape. Clothes lose their shape and look old before their time.

- Hang up a damp coat, but outside the closet until dry. Never put damp clothes into any closet.

- Button the top button or fastener, and zip the zipper to maintain proper shape.

- Straighten the garment on the hanger to preserve it's shape. All vertical seamlines should fall straight down. Slapping it carelessly on the hanger so one side hangs lower than the other takes a toll. Soon the garment won't hang straight on you.

- Resist the temptation to hang one garment over another. One garment per hanger is the rule or you'll pull both garments out of shape and lose track of what's underneath. Oh, you may think you'll remember, but you won't.

- Prevent stretching through the shoulders in quality dresses by adding long loops of seam tape anchored to front and back waistline seam, and then hanging the dress by the loops. These loops should be slightly shorter than waist to shoulder length to prevent stretching.

- Fold stretchy knit dresses and bias-cut dresses over a padded or full rounded hanger bar. Place the fold at the waist.

- Two-piece knit dresses, suits, skirts, and sweaters generally hold their shape better if they are folded flat and layered neatly on open shelves. Hang them up and they usually stretch out of shape. Stuff them in a drawer and they get scrunched and easily forgotten. You can also fold them in half then fold again, and carefully hang them over a padded hanger bar. Folding the knit lessens the strain that causes stretching.

- Sweaters can also be folded neatly over a padded hanger bar or towel bars mounted on sidewalls or the inside of the closet doors.

FIGURE 3.2
WITH EXPERIENCE YOU WILL BECOME BETTER ABLE TO LOOK AT ANY FIGURE, RECOGNIZE
THE GENERAL FIGURE TYPE, AND KNOW WHERE ATTENTION NEEDS TO BE DIRECTED.

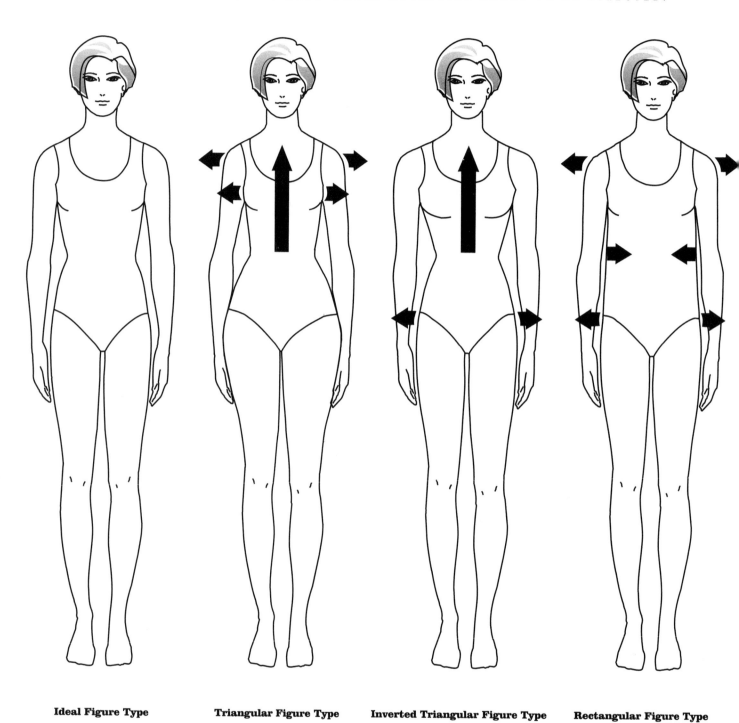

Ideal Figure Type   **Triangular Figure Type**   **Inverted Triangular Figure Type**   **Rectangular Figure Type**

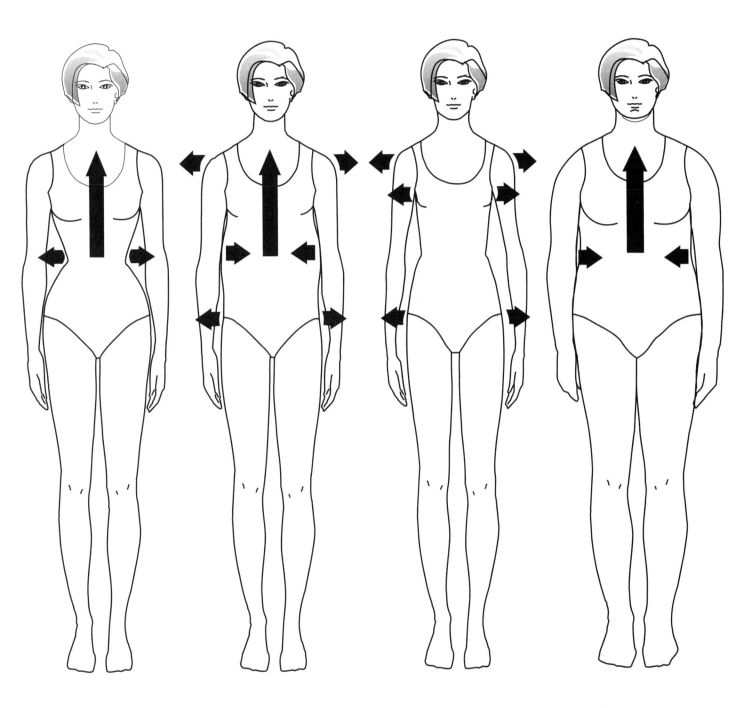

Hourglass Figure Type **Diamond-shaped Figure Type** **Tubular Figure Type** **Rounded Figure Type**

- To fold a sweater crease-free, lay it flat, front up, on the bed. Fold the sleeves across the upper chest, fold the bottom up over the sleeves. Periodically reverse the procedure.

- Hang, don't fold skirts over a hanger bar. The only exception is a knit straight skirt. Folding a gathered flared, or pleated skirt ruins its shape.

- Fold heavy beaded garments with layers of tissue paper to pad and prevent creases in these special treasures. Store on a shelf or in a drawer.

- Let shoes air thoroughly, about two hours, before putting them away.

- Stuff the toes of shoes with tissue or shoe trees to maintain or restore their shape.

- Stuff long cardboard tubes or large size magazines rolled up lengthwise into your boots. Boots will stand upright and keep their shape without excess wrinkles or cracking around the ankles. Commercial boot trees and boot shapers are also available for this purpose. Boots can also be hung on hooks using special boot clips.

- Pair up socks and roll neatly, then stand them in rows in a clear plastic box on the shelf.

- Don't crowd your clothes. Clothes smashed too close together come out wrinkled and misshapen.

- Brush garments, especially wool, to remove lint or surface soil. When possible, remove any spots or stains. These procedures help postpone washing or dry cleaning that may gradually distort the original shape of the garment.

- Rotate clothing between wearings. Wear once or twice, then give it a rest to allow body moisture and odor to fade, wrinkles to hang out and original shape to return.

- Hang wrinkled garments in the bathroom while you shower or bathe. This practice will steam out wrinkles and save you pressing time. To maintain the shape of jacket sleeves while steaming, gently stuff sleeves with a towel. Stuff more delicate blouse sleeves with tissue or clear plastic bags.

- Clean and press your clothes, but don't over-clean or press unnecessarily. With the possible exception of blouses or shirts, it is not necessary to wash or clean your clothes after every wearing. Each time you put clothes through the cleaning process you risk shrinkage, fading, loss of body and shape. The best suit is made to survive only 20 to 25 cleanings. Send it to the cleaner every 6 to 8 wearings and you'll kill it off before its time.

- Follow hangtag and garment care labels carefully!

- Put any extra thread, buttons or fabric pieces in a small plastic bag and hook the plastic bag over the hanger for ready access whenever needed.

Clothes Hangers

Clothes hangers come in a variety of shapes and materials. The proper hanger can preserve the original shape of a garment while the wrong hanger can ruin a garment.

Check the size of the hanger. Hangers need to be exactly wide enough to touch the shoulder seams. Any wider and they stretch the shoulder/sleeve area. The garment back stretches as it sags out of shape from collapsing on a hanger too narrow.

Wire Hangers

- Sturdy wire hangers are available at your local laundry at low cost. Not all wire hangers are rusty, thin and flimsy, ruin the shape of clothes, and snag fabric.
- Sturdy wire hangers are easy to handle, and are particularly easy to pack for travel. With the hanger left in the clothes, I can pack and unpack in minutes, always having enough hangers at my destination.
- Thin, flimsy wire hangers are suitable only for men's shirts that are worn once, then professionally laundered—they come with the laundered shirt.
- Wire hangers of heavier, smooth-coated metal wire support many clothes just fine. Look for those with a smooth shoulder slope.
- The minute a wire hanger gets bent out of shape or begins to discolor, get rid of it and get a new one.
- Use wire hangers under closely, firmly woven skirts, blouses, dresses, and light to medium weight jackets.
- Use wire hangers with a cardboard tube rolled over the base, for slacks. They don't leave a crease or hanger mark.

Plastic Hangers

- Tubular, plastic hangers are strong and hold the shape of your clothes only slightly better than wire. Watch out for rough edges that can snag clothes. They are too bulky to use in a suitcase.
- Molded plastic hangers are the type you often get from the store when you purchase a garment. They are ideal if you need to hook skirt waist loops onto the hanger. They break easily and are somewhat bulky in a suitcase.
- Foam-wrapped, molded plastic hangers are ideal for slippery silk or chiffon blouses, dresses, and light to medium-weight knits. Purchase a strip of foam rubber at the craft shop and wrap your own. They break easily under the weight of heavy clothes.

Decorative Hangers

- Brass, chrome, and tortoise shell hangers are expensive but elegant. Use them in your guest and coat closets.
- Matching and decorative hangers can be fun and pretty to own if the look is important to you. They are great for drip-dry clothes, especially when traveling.
- Padded, quilted hangers are beautiful and soft on the shape of most clothes, including knits, gowns, and party clothes. Padded hangers are generally too bulky to be used in a suitcase.

Wooden Hangers

- Recommended for tailored sport and suit jackets, coats for both men and women, and women's heavier weight dresses.
- Double-check the shoulder slope of the wooden hanger as compared to the shoulder slope of the garment. Even a wooden hanger can ruin the shape of a garment if the hanger shape is out of line.
- Watch out for rough edges and splinters. Poor quality wooden hangers aren't worth using.
- Even though they're heavy and bulky to travel with, take along one or two wooden hangers needed to hold the shape of a good jacket or dress.
- Plastic or wooden suit-hangers are fine for men's suits, but are not recommended for women's suits. Skirts hung under a jacket tend to sag at the center. Hidden under a jacket, you won't think of wearing the skirt with other tops. It is better to hang them separately.

Skirt Hangers

- Skirt hangers, made of wire, plastic, or wood, all have metal clamps or clips that leave pressure marks in fabric and suede.
- Protect a garment from clip marks by placing a small piece of medium to heavyweight fabric as a pad between the garment waistband and the clips.
- Plastic skirt hangers work well, but break easily. If suitable, wooden are your best bet.
- Many skirt hangers are too narrow to adequately support the full width and weight of a skirt. Consider using a sturdy wire hanger and three clothespins. While it may be unattractive, skirts are well supported and won't sag off grain or fold at the center as they do with many commercial skirt hangers that have only two clips. If the skirt is particularly heavy, use four clothespins.

Trouser Hangers

- Wooden trouser hangers are great for men's trousers and women's slacks. Hang trousers and slacks from the waist or the hem.
- Trouser hangers also work well for light to medium-weight flared skirts.
- Avoid trouser hangers with a swing-out metal bar. The bar pops out just when you don't want it too and leaves crease marks on trousers and slacks.
- Multiple garment hangers for blouses, shirts, pants, skirts and scarves save space by hanging one garment above another in vertical row of four to six garments, but don't use them unless you're really cramped for space. They leave crease marks on pants and clip marks on waistbands. Skirts are often too heavy and slip out. Skirts get crushed and the bottom garment often hangs on the floor.

Chapter 4
How to Improve the Fit

Standards of fit vary from person to person, place to place and time to time. One woman may spend hours to get her clothes perfectly custom cut to fit. Another woman may be happy with ready-to-wear clothes quickly altered in-store to fit. And still another may be satisfied with clothes straight from the rack regardless of whether they fit or not. One cultural group may believe that good fit means two inches of ease in the seat, and another may demand four or more. Still another cultural group may ban body conscious silhouettes. Use the guidelines or standards discussed in this chapter to evaluate and judge the fit of your clothes—to compare actual fit with a fabulous fit and pinpoint areas of poor fit. You'll never again be confused by a fashion magazine or catalog that features an outfit that doesn't fit, or give in to an overzealous salesperson engaged in flattery to make a sale. You'll know what you're looking for and how to find it.

What Is a Fabulous Fit?

Underwear bands and straps must not cut into the body and show through clothes.

Necklines should fit the curve around the base of the neck, unless designed to do otherwise, without cutting into the neck, wrinkling or gapping. A wide or lowered neckline should lie flat and snug on the body.

Collars and Neckbands should fit the neck comfortably snug unless designed to do otherwise. When buttoned at the neck, one finger should fit easily into a shirt collar. A suit collar should reveal about 1/2" of a shirt collar at center back. The outer edge of the suit collar should just cover the neckline seam.

Lapels should lie symmetrical and flat without gapping open.

Shoulder Seams should lie on top of the shoulder, appear to bisect the neck and shoulder, and end at the shoulder joint unless designed to do otherwise. Shoulder pads should be well placed, appear natural, not too large or lumpy.

Armhole Seamlines should cross the shoulder at the shoulder joint (end of the collar bone) unless designed to do otherwise. The seamline will appear in line with the back arm crease. A jacket armhole seam may extend 1/2" to 1" beyond the shoulder joint and a coat 1" to 1 1/2" beyond.

Armholes should be large enough to allow for easy movement without cutting into the arm, binding or gapping. The lowest point should lie 1" to 2" below the armpit unless designed to do otherwise.

Upper Back areas should lie smooth, without wrinkles or strain at the armhole seam when arms are forward. There should be no horizontal wrinkle, bubble or bulge below the collar.

Darts should point toward, and end about 1" to 1 1/2" from the fullest part of the body curve being fitted, with no wrinkles or bubble at the dart tip. The larger the curve, the larger the dart must be and vice versa.

"Let's face it, most of us dislike fitting. But without the correct fit, our clothes just hang in the closet, unworn."

NANCY ZIEMAN
NANCY'S NOTIONS LTD.

Center Front and Back Seams should be centered on the body and fall straight down, perpendicular to the floor. They should not shift or pull to the side.

Closures should hang straight and smooth, without wrinkles or gapping across the chest, bust, back, abdomen or hip area. A front button closure needs a button at bust level.

Side Seams should extend from the center of the underarm straight down, perpendicular to the floor. They should not shift or pull to the front or back. Side seams should appear to intersect the waistline at a 90 degree angle.

Lengthwise Grain (vertical fabric threads) should fall straight down the center front or center back, perpendicular to the floor, unless fabric is cut on the bias (diagonal grain). Lengthwise grain also hangs down the center of a sleeve above the elbow and down the crease of slacks or trousers.

Crosswise Grain (horizontal fabric threads) should be parallel to the floor at the chest, upper back, upper arm, hip and hem unless cut on the bias (diagonal grain).

Set-in Sleeve Caps should lie at the end of the shoulder and curve smoothly around the armhole, without puckers or wrinkles. Fullness should be evenly distributed, front and back.

Sleeves should be large enough to lie smooth around the arm with about 1 1/2" ease. One finger should fit easily under a short sleeve hem. Ease at the elbow should be sufficient to allow the arm to bend without binding. Elbow darts or fullness should be centered over the end of the bone when the arm is bent.

Short Sleeve Length should appear attractive in proportion to the chest or bust and to the total arm length.

Long Sleeve Length should end at the wrist bone when the arm is bent upward at the elbow—when arms are down at your sides, long sleeves should hang no longer than the bend of the wrist. The shirt sleeve cuff should show about 1/2" below a suit or sport jacket sleeve, for men and women.

Pockets should lie closed and flat against the body unless styled to extend away.

Waistbands and waisted dresses should fit comfortably snug at the natural waistline when standing, yet remain comfortable when sitting. Two fingers should slip easily inside a waistband.

Gathers should be tiny and evenly spaced, with no bulges or spaces. They should fall straight down or radiate evenly from a seamline.

Vents, Slits, Pleats and Tucks should hang straight, flat, closed and smooth against the body when standing, not gap or pull open. They should open only with movement.

Jackets should fit loose enough to ease comfortably over a shirt, blouse or sweater. Traditionally, suit jackets and sport coats should cover the seat of men's slacks. Jackets should not pull tight around the abdomen or hips when fastened.

Coats should fit loose enough to ease comfortably over a jacket or suit worn underneath.

Skirts should fit loosely enough for fabric to relax and lie smooth on the body. There should be 2" minimum wearing ease. There should be no horizontal fold or crease around the waist, below the waist at center back, or at the hip joint (break in the leg). Skirts should taper or fall straight down below the abdomen and hipline, not cup or cut under the stomach, thighs or buttocks.

Pants and Trousers should fit smoothly over the abdomen, buttocks and thighs, with adequate seat fullness and crotch length. Slacks should not hang below or cut up into the crotch area. There should be no wrinkles that radiate from the crotch area. There should be no horizontal fold around the waist or below the waist at center back.

Linings should fit smoothly and comfortably loose.

Hems should form an even line all around, parallel to the floor, unless designed to do otherwise. The folds of circular, flared or draped skirts should fall into place in an even line.

Skirt Hems should not cross at the widest part of the calf. Classic skirt length is 2" to 2 1/2" below the center of the knee, or in other words, just above the calf curve. Lengths longer or shorter depend on the style and fabric of the skirt. They should be in proportion to the entire figure and flatter the leg.

Pants and Trouser Hems should brush the top of the shoe in front, the top of the heel in back or taper slightly lower in back, unless designed to do otherwise.

Coat Hems should cover or fall about 1" longer than skirts and extend past the pants or trouser seat or below.

Analyze the Wrinkles

Wrinkles give you clues to poor fit. A fitting wrinkle indicates that something doesn't fit properly. There is either too little or too much fabric. You can't iron out fitting wrinkles. They simply reappear. Don't confuse fitting wrinkles with folds in the fabric that are part of the design—folds that result from gathers, tucks, flare, etc.—or with wrinkles that come from moving about. Some wrinkles may be caused by poor posture. Improve the posture and you improve the fit. Wrinkles disappear. Wrinkles are to be expected when you walk, bend, reach, etc. When you stop moving and stand still, clothing should settle smoothly over your body. If the clothing settles into wrinkles, they're probably fitting wrinkles and there are two types, tight and loose.

Tight Wrinkles form when the fabric is strained because there is not enough fabric.

Tight horizontal wrinkles generally indicate the clothes are too small around—too narrow. If possible, fabric will shift to a smaller area. The garment needs to be wider or let out at the vertical seam(s).

Tight vertical wrinkles usually signal the clothes are too short. The garment needs to be longer or let down at the nearest horizontal seam.

Tight diagonal wrinkles are a clue that the garment is too small—too narrow and/or too short—for the body bulge or contour above the wrinkles. Instead of a diagonal wrinkle, fabric may bow upward. The body contour is large or prominent. The garment needs to be larger or let out at both the vertical and horizontal seams.

Loose Wrinkles form when the fabric sags. There is too much fabric.

Loose horizontal wrinkles usually mean the garment is too long. The garment needs to be shorter or taken up at the horizontal seam(s).

Loose vertical wrinkles indicate the garment is large around—too wide. The garment needs to be narrower or taken in at the nearest vertical seam.

Loose, droopy curves or the downward sag of fabric signal the garment is both too long and too wide for the body contour above it. The body contour is small or shallow. The garment needs to be smaller or taken in at both the horizontal and vertical seams.

Adapt To Fit

When you realize a garment does not fit or flatter your figure the way it should, look for ways to change the way it fits or looks. Add or replace ill-fitting shoulder pads to lift and improve top to bottom balance and proportion, or adjust the length of the sleeves by rolling them up neatly. Some clothes come with built-in versatility that allow you to adapt them to fit. The appearance of a well-fitted but less flattering style may be improved by layering with another, more flattering piece of clothing.

Re-check the fit of your clothes periodically, particularly if your weight has changed. If a garment has stretched out of shape due to cleaning or wear and tear, get rid of it. Wear only what looks good on you.

Alter to Fit

Alteration is the process of changing particular parts of a garment to fit a particular person. With minor adjustments made by someone who knows what he or she is doing, the garment can look as if it were custom-made. Successful alterations depend on knowing when to alter and when not to alter, where to begin and how to proceed. Don't be misled by an optimistic tailor—not all garments or all areas on a garment can be altered effectively. On the other hand, if you are told the alteration is impossible, accept it. No tailor can take in a size 16 to fit a size 12 figure or let out a size 8 to fit a size 14 frame.

When Not To Alter

Almost anything can be taken apart and put back together to fit, but you need a miracle worker to do it and the job will be costly because of the work involved. The only exception might be if you found a fantastic garment at a fantastic price, the alteration is feasible and worth the time and expense.

Even then, consider carefully if you find yourself in any of the following situations:

• If you aren't completely happy with the style of the garment, don't expect alterations to make everything wonderful. Alterations to change the style of a garment are risky at best and require exceptional skill. Rather than plan on altering the style of brand new clothes, look for something else that better suits your personal style.

• Alterations to the neckline, collar, shoulder and armhole areas of a garment are generally not recommended. These tricky adjustments set up a chain reaction of other fitting problems. On occasion, a competent tailor will raise or lower the collar on a jacket. Rarely do you alter the shoulder area of a jacket or coat, especially one with shoulder pads.

• A garment that requires extensive, multiple, alterations will likely never fit properly.

• Alterations that require crossing several seams are difficult. Simpler styles offer you a better chance of success.

• Alterations that interfere with dominant design lines or proportions of the garment are likewise not advised. This can be the case if the garment is more than one size too small or too large.

• Regardless of style, satin and moiré finish fabrics, vinyl, leather, and suede can't be altered because the holes punched from previous stitching lines remain in the fabric.

• Telltale marks from original seam, fold, and hemlines will show in synthetic knits, velvet, velveteen, velour, suede cloth, and corduroy. Silk and other lightweight blouse and dress fabrics may have been weakened by original stitching and may also show signs of restitching.

• Clothes with a heat-set or permanent press finish can't be altered because the folds of original creases, seam and hemlines can never be completely removed or reset.

• Even in new clothing, exposed fabric may have faded and covered areas, such as seam allowances or pleat underlays, may be a shade darker when they're let out. Check a small area before making major changes.

• If a new garment is spotted or soiled, it must be cleaned before altering. Pressing during alteration will set the soil into the fabric, making it permanent.

• Plaid, stripe and check fabrics don't lend themselves easily to alteration because the lines may never match up after the seams are shifted.

• Clothes with narrow or slashed seam allowances lack the necessary fabric to be let out. If you plan to let out a seam, make sure there's a generous seam allowance. If not enough, I recommend you buy a size larger and take it in.

• Garments with sequin, bead or braid trimming within the area to be adjusted cannot be altered unless the trim is available to replace any trim removed during the alteration.

Guidelines for a Fabulous Fit

Guidelines that apply to altering clothes in the store apply to altering at home:

• **Wear appropriate underwear and shoes during the fitting.**

• **Fit the garment right side out. Many people have figure variations that differ from one side of their body to the other—the figure is asymmetrical. This will also help you visualize how the altered garment will look.**

• **Fit the garment with all closures fastened. If the garment has a belt, fit it with the belt in place. The alterationist will help you in-store. Have a friend help if you're at home.**

• **If the garment is new, it may shrink the first time it is cleaned. Consider cleaning or allowing for shrinkage before altering. If the store alters a garment and the garment shrinks, return to the store and insist that the alteration be redone with no additional charge.**

• **When possible, especially in the case of an expensive garment, make one major alteration at a time and try the garment on before making another alteration. In some cases, the first alteration may correct another fitting problem as well. Insist on a second fitting session.**

• **Because clothing hangs from the top of the garment, begin fitting at the top and work down. Avoid too much fitting. Later, execute alterations from the top and work down.**

• **Maintain fitting standards when altering—maintain proper grainline and seamline positions, good balance, amounts of ease, etc.**

• **Avoid drastic alterations in any one place. You run the risk of ruining the style lines. When possible, distribute the amount of change between several darts or seams.**

• **Alter vertical seams before horizontal seams. Do hemlines last. Each alteration affects the other. The hang of the hem will depend on the total fit of the pressed garment.**

• **Press often, after each step of the alteration is completed and particularly before crossing a seam with another sewing line.**

• **If seams are taken in, leave very generous seam allowances, in case the seams must be let out again.**

• **Keep leftover thread and fabric. You never know when that fabric might be needed to repair the garment.**

TABLE 4.1
GUIDELINES FOR A FABULOUS FIT

When To Alter

Alterations in size are generally the most successful. There are two types of size alterations. The first type includes alterations made when your body measurements differ from standard measurements. Changing the length of a basic skirt, pant or sleeve is relatively easy. Taking in the waist or letting out the hip and thigh area are a bit more difficult, and shortening crotch depth in slacks or trousers is still more difficult. The second type includes alterations on curved areas that can't be measured with a tape, such as altering for a sway back, flat buttocks, or raising the crotch curve. The only way to analyze the fit and need for alteration is to see how the garment hangs and pulls on your body. In many instances the alteration cannot be done because the fabric has already been cut.

Alterations can generally be carried out on suit jackets, sport coats and blazers, raincoats, topcoats or overcoats, slacks or trousers, skirts and medium-weight dresses. Alterations on shirts and blouses are questionable because of cost, although sleeves down around your knuckles look ridiculous. The number of custom shirt shops and catalog companies that offer shirts and blouses altered or cut to fit is growing to meet the need.

Better department and fine clothing stores employ an alterationist—a tailor or seamstress. A few specialty stores contract with a private alterationist. Whether you use an in-store tailor, your own tailor or work with a friend to do the alteration yourself, the following guidelines will result in a great fit.

• Ask for the alterationist, not the store salesperson, to carry out the fitting. He or she should place the marks or pins that will guide the work that follows.

• Ask about the cost of in-store alterations before arranging to have them done. Often there is no charge for basic alterations in men's wear but alterations to women's wear are often extra. You don't want to be caught by surprise after the fact. Prices vary too much to quote. Alterations on plaids, pleats, lined garments, leather and suede often cost more. Ask if price is per piece or per hour. A set price per piece or procedure is usually better. You are not expected to tip. If alteration costs mount to forty dollars or more, you probably ought to reconsider.

• Ask how long it will be before you can pick up your altered clothes. In some stores, minor alterations can be made immediately and you can take the item home, ready to wear. Unless you have an immediate need and the store can work it into their schedule, allow two to seven days or up to two weeks for more complicated alterations.

• If you're without an in-store alterationist or the necessary skills to do the job yourself, start scouting for an independent tailor or seamstress. Look in the yellow pages of your telephone book. Contact the fashion department at the local college or trade school. Check the nearest chapter of the American Sewing Guild. Ask at fabric stores and dry cleaners for names. Ask friends and associates for their recommendations. If they are pleased with some-

one's work, chances are you will be too. Ask for references. Ask to see examples of their work and a price sheet. A good alterationist is worth what you pay. Request the following procedures at the same time:

• Check all buttons and snaps to make sure they are secure. Reinforce or reattach if necessary.

• Remove any tag-end threads and unnecessary belt loops, particularly string loops.

• On expensive items, if unusual or self-fabric covered buttons are used, request the store to order an extra button for you. This will save you time and money if you lose a button later.

• When you go to pick up your altered garment, don't leave the store without trying the garment on to check the fit. Walk, sit, and move around. If not satisfied, say so and insist that the alteration be corrected.

• If the cost is more than you're willing to pay, and you have the necessary time and sewing skills, the alterationist can mark or pin the amounts of change for you and you can complete the alteration at home. Just don't gamble with an expensive outfit to save ten or fifteen dollars. Money spent to upgrade the fit and look of your clothes is money well spent.

Custom Cut to Fit

If you continually have a difficult time getting good fit in your clothes, you should consider having your clothes custom made for you—at least some of them. It may be the only way you will ever get the fit and quality you want in your clothes.

The cost of custom-made clothes varies. They may cost no more than what you'd pay for ready-made clothes plus alterations—maybe less. On the other hand, you are paying for a specialized service and one-of-a-kind garments, so the cost can be somewhat more. Other factors also enter in, such as the area of the country where you live, the state of the local economy, along with the experience and reputation of the professional. A prestigious tailor or dressmaker located in the high-rent district will charge significantly more than someone less well known who works in-home.

With custom-made clothes, the design or pattern is altered to your exact measurements before the fabric is ever cut. You can expect a tailor to work more with jackets and trousers. A dressmaker tends to work on more softly styled clothes. You may select from a stock of patterns, bring a commercial pattern with you, have something you already own copied, or have something original designed especially for you.

When finding a professional tailor or dressmaker, consider word-of-mouth recommendations from satisfied customers among your best bets. Visit or call the fabric shops in your area and ask if they can recommend someone for you. A good shop will have a list of dressmakers who have brought in samples of their work so that store personnel know the quality of work. Other shops may simply have a list or file of business cards, but know little about the quality of work. Dry-cleaning establishments and department stores may also have names. You can also check your telephone book yellow pages and newspaper service ads.

Once in contact with a tailor or dressmaker, ask for references and samples. Discuss patterns, fabric, fittings, and delivery time. All of these factors will affect final price. Be open to suggestions but remember you are the one who has to make the final decisions. Get a price or price range before you commit yourself. If you have doubts about this being the right course for you, start by having a less costly garment made for you, such as a skirt or simple blouse. This will also give you time to become acquainted and comfortable with this individual. It works both ways, and gives the tailor or dressmaker time to become familiar with your figure and any fitting problems. "Before long," agrees Lorraine Henry, Conselle consultant and custom dressmaker for twenty years, "your dressmaker will know your figure type and its variations better than you do." When you are satisfied that she/he knows how to do business and you can work well together, then the sky—or your budget—is the limit. You'll probably find that the two of you will become best of friends.

Having your clothes custom cut and sewn takes time—more time than it usually takes to go to the store and buy something off the rack. The time is well spent, however, if the clothes fit. So plan ahead. Plan on two to four sessions to go from pattern selection to measurement taking, to fitting, and then to finished garment. More complicated styles take more fittings. Allow yourself at least two weeks to a month if possible, depending on the garment style and dressmaker's schedule. Custom clothes are better not rushed. Unlike retail, you can't take an item back if you don't like it. Make sure you get what you want—a fabulous fit.

Mirror, Mirror. How can I look better? How can I learn to dress better? How can I get my clothes to fit better?

These are age old questions. My instant and unrehearsed recommendation? Look in the mirror—a full-length mirror. While you view your face in the mirror over the bathroom sink daily, there's a lot happening from the neck down! Many women never see themselves full-length or from behind. You would make fewer fashion mistakes if you looked at yourself front, back and both side views not only when shopping, but later at home and before leaving to go out.

I know, it can be pretty depressing for some of us to come face to face with reality in our underwear in front of a full-length mirror. That's when I wish I didn't like double-chocolate-decadence quite so much, and that I'd begun a regular exercise program about twenty years earlier. It's that kind of reality, however, that you need to make sure your clothes fit and flatter your figure.

Blouses and Shirts

Stand facing a full-length mirror, with your arms relaxed at your sides.

❏ Yes ❏ No
Does the neckline, neckband, or collar fit the curve around your neck, not gap or cut in uncomfortably?

❏ Yes ❏ No
Does the neckline, neckband, or collar lie smooth at the base of your neck, front, sides, and back?

❏ Yes ❏ No
Can you wear the collar more than one way—turned up, down, buttoned, unbuttoned? If you can't button the top button, the collar is too tight.

❏ Yes ❏ No
Do shoulder seams bisect the shoulder—lie straight, directly on top of the shoulder?

❏ Yes ❏ No
Do the armhole seams cross over or just outside the end of your shoulder joint (collar bone)? If they cross on the inside, the shoulder area of the garment is too narrow. Padded shoulders and drop-shoulder designs may extend beyond.

❏ Yes ❏ No
Do closures lie flat and smooth without gapping or pulling open at chest, bust, or hips? If a closure gaps or pulls open, the blouse is too small.

❏ Yes ❏ No
If the shirt is fitted, do the darts point toward and end slightly before the fullest part of the bust?

❏ Yes ❏ No
If the blouse is sleeveless, do the armholes bind or cut into your underarm? If they do, the blouse is too small. Do they gap, allowing a side view inside your blouse? If they do, the blouse is too large.

❏ Yes ❏ No
Is the set-in sleeve cap smoothly rounded, free of puckers or wrinkles? A gathered sleeve cap has gathers evenly distributed.

❏ Yes ❏ No
Are short sleeves loose enough to slip your fingers easily between the fabric and your arm? Bend your arms upward from the elbow, parallel to the floor.

❏ Yes ❏ No
If the sleeves are long, can you bend your elbows easily? Elbow darts should be centered over the end of the bone when the arm is bent.

❏ Yes ❏ No
Are long sleeves, including cuffs, long enough? If sleeves don't reach your wrist bone when cuffs are closed, they are too short. If sleeves lie below your wrist bone, they are too long. Raise your arms and bring them around in front of your chest.

❏ Yes ❏ No
Does the fabric feel strained or pull across the back of the blouse, as if it might rip? If it does, the blouse is too small. Raise your arms above your head, as if combing your hair. Are the sleeves comfortably loose?

❏ Yes ❏ No
Is the shirt tail long enough to stay tucked neatly into your skirt, slacks, or trousers? If the shirt pulls out of your waistband it is too short. Twist around, bend over and generally move around.

❏ Yes ❏ No
Does the shirt or blouse feel comfortable as you move? Four extra inches of ease around the waist are recommended for a comfortable fit, so you can "pinch an inch" on each side.

❏ Yes ❏ No
If the blouse has a scoop or lowered neckline, does it fit closely or fall away from the body when you bend over?

Note: The appearance of a well-fitted but less flattering neckline or collar, sleeve, blouse, or shirt may be improved by layering with another, more flattering piece of clothing, such as a scarf, vest, sweater, or jacket. Shoulder pads added to appropriate blouse or shirt styles may increase your options.

Skirts

Stand in front of a full-length mirror, with your weight balanced over both feet.

❏ Yes ❏ No
Can you fasten the waistband easily?

❏ Yes ❏ No
Does the waistband fit comfortably snug, with room to slip two fingers easily inside the band? If not, the waistband is uncomfortably small and will not accommodate a blouse tucked in.

❏ Yes ❏ No
Does the waistband gap or drop below the waist to rest on the hips? If so, it is too large.

❏ Yes ❏ No
Does the waistband lie flat? If the waistband buckles or folds over, it is too wide.

❏ Yes ❏ No
Does the skirt closure lie closed and smooth, without wrinkling or gapping?

❏ Yes ❏ No
Are hip darts well positioned over the abdomen or buttocks, angled slightly outward, and tapered to a point without puckers? If darts pucker at the bottom, they are too large. If they end below the hipline, they are too long.

❏ Yes ❏ No
Are center front and back seams centered on the body and perpendicular to the floor? If they shift or pull toward one side, the skirt may be too small on that side or be cut off grain.

❏ Yes ❏ No
Do the side seams appear to bisect the body and hang straight down perpendicular to the floor? If the seam pulls to the front or the back, that half of the skirt may be too small around that area.

❏ Yes ❏ No
Does the skirt slip or shift around the body, positioning seams out of place? If so, the skirt may be too loose.

❏ Yes ❏ No
Does the skirt ride up, forming a fold of fabric just below your waist? If so, the skirt is too small around the high or low hip area. If you have to pull the skirt down to keep it in place, that's another sign the skirt is too small.

❏ Yes ❏ No
Does the skirt hang straight down below the fullest area of your stomach, hips, thighs, or buttocks? If skirt cups under, it is too small.

❏ Yes ❏ No
Do pleats, tucks, vents, and slits lie closed and smooth while standing?

❏ Yes ❏ No
Do skirt pockets lie closed, without gapping or pulling open? Where does the hemline cross your leg? Skirt lengths above or below the widest part of the calf are most flattering to the leg, but should be in flattering proportion to the entire figure. Is the skirt hem even all the way around—parallel to the floor? If the hem pulls up in front, back or at the side, that area of the skirt is too short.

Sit down.

❏ Yes ❏ No
Is the waistband pulled uncomfortably tight and the fastener strained?

❏ Yes ❏ No
Are the seams strained to the ripping point?

❏ Yes ❏ No
Does the skirt ride up drastically? Bend over, walk around. Does the waistband pull down drastically in back when you bend or kneel down?

❏ Yes ❏ No
Can you walk easily?

❏ Yes ❏ No
If the skirt has a slit at side or back, does it reveal too much leg when you walk?

❏ Yes ❏ No
Does the skirt wrinkle, ripple or ride up as you move around? Two to four extra inches of ease around the hip area is recommended for a comfortable fit. You can "pinch an inch" on each side.

Note: By wearing a jacket, sweater, or vest that creates a transitional line from shoulder to hip, concealing the waist/hip area, you can often increase your skirt options.

Pants and Trousers

Check the fitting points listed for skirt waistbands, closures and seam lines.

❏ Yes   ❏ No
Are trouser pleats long enough and/or full enough to hang straight down below the stomach?

❏ Yes   ❏ No
Do slacks or trousers fit smoothly over the abdomen, buttocks and thighs and hang straight down below the fullest part? If they pull tight across or cup under the abdomen, buttocks, or thighs, they are too small. (Fashion pants may fit differently, according to design.)

❏ Yes   ❏ No
Do pockets lie closed and flat against the body? If they pull open, the pants are too small.

❏ Yes   ❏ No
Do pants have adequate seat fullness and crotch length? If pants hang loosely below the crotch, they are too long in the body. If pants wrinkle or cut up into the crotch area, they are too short in the body.

❏ Yes   ❏ No
Does the hem edge fall in the proper place? Straight leg slacks should brush the top of the shoe in front, the heel in back or taper slightly longer in back. If pants are pegged or tapered at the hem, they should be hemmed at the ankle or above. If pants are flared, they may hang nearly to the floor. Sit and kneel down.

❏ Yes   ❏ No
Does the waistband stay level? If it pulls down in the back, the body of the pant is too short.

❏ Yes   ❏ No
Do pants bind or cut up into the crotch area? If so, pants are too short in the body.

Note: By wearing an appropriate jacket or top that creates a transitional line from shoulder to hip, you may improve the appearance of slacks or trousers.

Sweaters, Jackets, and Vests

Check the fitting points for blouses and shirts. Stand in front of a full-length mirror, with your weight balanced over both feet.

❏ Yes   ❏ No
Can you pull a crewneck or turtleneck sweater easily over your head?

❏ Yes   ❏ No
Does the jacket wrinkle or bulge just below the collar across the back? If so, the upper back is too long—the neck curve is too high.

❏ Yes   ❏ No
Is there adequate ease or dart shaping across the back shoulder area to allow a smooth fit over the shoulder blades?

❏ Yes   ❏ No
Does the jacket fit smoothly across the upper chest and bust? If a diagonal or vertical fold forms between the shoulder and bust, the jacket is too small across the chest and bust.

❏ Yes   ❏ No
Do lapels lie symmetrically on the body?

❏ Yes   ❏ No
Are low-hip-length jackets, sweaters and vests long enough to cover the widest part of your hips, buttocks, and thighs? Do jacket vents or the center back pleat hang straight, flat and closed?

❏ Yes   ❏ No
Do pockets lie closed, without gapping or pulling open?

❏ Yes   ❏ No
Do jacket sleeves allow about $1/2$" of the blouse or shirt sleeve to show below the hem? Move around, raise your arms, swing your arms back and forth.

❏ Yes   ❏ No
Is the jacket, sweater, or vest styled large enough to fit easily and comfortably over a blouse, shirt, or dress underneath? Is the armhole cut full enough to raise your arms above your head without straining the seams?

Note: A softly-gathered skirt, flared skirt or loosely-styled pants may increase your jacket, sweater and vest options.

Coats

Check the appropriate fitting points for blouses, shirts, skirts, dresses, and jackets, as they may apply to the fit of a coat. Double check sleeve length. Stand in front of a full-length mirror with weight balanced over both feet.

❑ Yes   ❑ No
Do the shoulder seams of set-in sleeves extend $1/2$" to $1 1/2$" beyond the natural shoulder—below the curve of the shoulder if designed with a drop shoulder?

❑ Yes   ❑ No
Does the coat wrinkle or bulge just below the collar across the back? If so, the upper back is too long—the neck curve is too high.

❑ Yes   ❑ No
Does the coat hang smoothly from shoulder to hem?

❑ Yes   ❑ No
Is the coat hemmed long enough to cover your skirt?

❑ Yes   ❑ No
Do coat sleeves cover shirt and jacket sleeves? Coat sleeves should be about $1/2$" longer than jacket sleeves, just covering the wrist bone when your arms hang relaxed at your sides. Move around and swing your arms back and forth.

❑ Yes   ❑ No
Is the coat styled large enough to fit easily and comfortably over clothes worn underneath, and still allow you to move freely?

❑ Yes   ❑ No
Is there enough room in coat pockets to hold your hands inside?

Dresses

Check the fitting points listed for blouses, shirts, and skirts, because a dress combines the two.

❑ Yes   ❑ No
Does the dress waistline encircle or lie at your natural waistline? If the waistline lies above or below, the dress is respectively too short or too long in the bodice.

❑ Yes   ❑ No
If the dress is styled without a waistline—chemise, princess, empire, drop-waist, etc.—is there enough ease around the waist for fabric to lie smoothly?

Chapter 5
The Seam Method of
Pattern Alteration

When you cannot get a satisfactory fit in clothes from the stores or catalogs, it is time to turn to home sewn or custom sewn clothing with patterns altered to fit your figure. Further refinements can be made during construction of the garment. If you do not enjoy sewing for yourself or you do not have the necessary skills, seek the skills of a professional dressmaker or tailor. Even then, not all sewing professionals use the most accurate and efficient method of pattern alteration.

Alteration Standards

Finished pattern alterations must meet the following standards for accuracy:

- The amounts of change must be correct.
- The style of the garment must be the same as before the alteration, unless a style change was intentional.
- The straight-of-grain line or arrow must be positioned the same as before the alteration so the fabric hangs or drapes properly.
- Center front and center back seamlines or foldlines must be straight.
- Curved seams must curve smoothly.
- Adjoining seam seamlines must match.
- The altered pattern must lie smooth and flat. If the pattern is puffy, bubbly, puckered or wrinkled in any area, size will be smaller in that area.

Most home sewers and professionals still depend on the traditional slash method of pattern alteration. Traditional slash procedures position alterations internally—the pattern is cut apart in the area of the actual figure variation. This is logical, but often causes distortion at the edge of the pattern. Many slash method procedures still do not solve the fitting problem but actually create more problems because of distortion. The pattern appears ruined when cut through the middle. Problems are compounded if there is more than one alteration on a pattern piece.

Two other methods, the pivot method and the seam method, position alterations at the seamline. When an alteration is positioned at the seamline, there is less distortion from original shape. Changes in outline, dart size, and shape are simple and accurate. Few sewers have mastered the more advanced pivot method—one that allows them to alter the pattern while cutting out the fabric. And few are acquainted with the new seam method.

All methods produce identical results—as they should. *Fabulous Fit* presents only the seam method of alteration because the method is generally accurate, quick, and easy for beginners as well as experienced professionals. It does not turn the pattern into a jigsaw puzzle of pieces. Even if you do not intend to alter patterns yourself, you can share the seam method and procedures that apply to your figure with the sewing professional you plan to work with.

"Consider pattern changes a part of the creative process…and you will enjoy the results more."

SANDRA BETZINA
POWER SEWING

General Concept

Using the seam method of alteration, you cut from the point where a figure variation begins, to the point where the variation ends—between the points where your figure does not measure to fit the pattern. These points are called "pivot points."

Next, spread the free seam allowance away from the pattern or overlap it onto the pattern. This changes the size and/or shape of the affected area. While you see the change at the edge of the pattern, the effect is incorporated within the body of the pattern, just where it is needed. In the case of multisized patterns without marked seamlines, simply cut the pattern in from the edge the specified seam allowance amount (traditionally 5/8").

More than one seam allowance is often involved in an alteration. For example, when you alter for a rounded upper back, you cut the back neck and the shoulder seam allowances free because both areas are affected. The variation is greatest at the center of the back and usually ends at the end of the shoulders. It is possible, however, that the shoulders are also rounded or sloped. If so, you also cut the armhole seam allowance free. That is the beauty of the seam method. You can alter for combined figure variations easily and without changing the original length of the seamline unless you need to.

Step-By-Step Pattern Alteration

A successful pattern alteration demands an orderly, step-by-step procedure, according to general alteration principles or guidelines. Take your time and work carefully.

1. Find a clean counter, table or desk to work on. Portable cardboard and corkboard surfaces can be nice to work on. They are available at many fabric or sewing machine stores.

2. Gather the supplies and tools you need.

    • Pattern

    • Tissue or other light-weight, plain paper

    • Scissors

    • Transparent tape. Reusable tape is now available.

    • Soft-lead pencils. Pencil lines in red make alterations easy to find.

    • Note paper

    • Straight-edge and curved rulers. Clear plastic rulers allow you to see pattern markings underneath.

3. Prepare the pattern.

    • Press the pattern with a warm, dry iron—steam can cause shrinkage. A wrinkled pattern decreases size and accuracy.

- Reinforce the pattern for a firmer, more durable surface to work on. Apply light-weight, fusible interfacing to the underside of the pattern. Keep both paper and interfacing perfectly smooth.

- Cut out the pattern—carefully.

4. Double check the amount(s) of change needed. This is the difference (+ or -) between your body measurement and the pattern measurement including the appropriate amount of ease allowed by the designer. If the amount of change is more than 2 inches, you may be smart to choose another size or another style better suited to your figure type.

5. Think through each alteration individually. One alteration may affect adjoining pattern pieces and other alterations will need to be made. Make any notes you need for now or later when you want to make the same alteration on a similar pattern.

6. Plan alterations working from the top of the pattern down, in the following order:

- Even amounts of change in length.
- Uneven amounts of change in length/contour.
- Even amounts of change in width.
- Uneven amounts of change in width/contour.

Changes above affect the fit below. When the lengthwise position is corrected, the width may be just fine. Even amounts of change are easier to make than uneven amounts. Start simple.

When altering for a change in circumference, divide the total amount of change by the number of seams affected. This distributes the amount of change evenly among the seam edges. For example, if a skirt in two pieces (front and back) is 2" too small, divide 2" by the four seam edges affected. Distribute the result, 1/2", among each seam edge.

FIGURE 5.1
EXAMPLES OF THE SEAM METHOD FOR A LARGER BUST.

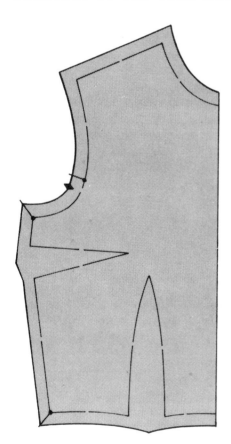

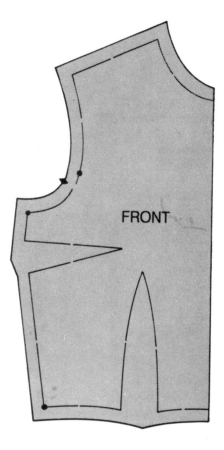

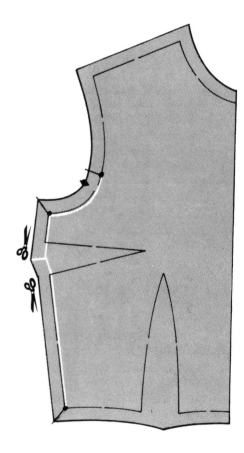

A Mark pivot points.

B Draw a line across the seam allowance at each pivot point.

C Cut the affected seam allowance free from the pattern, just inside the stitching line.

7. Plan for any corresponding alterations. Alterations on one pattern piece may demand an alteration on an adjoining pattern piece so that seamlines match.

8. Place the pattern with printed side up, on top of alteration paper.

9. Locate the seamline to be altered, the one affected by the figure variation.

10. Identify and mark pivot points on the seamline at the following points. (See step A.)

   • At the point where the figure variation begins.

   • At the point where the figure variation ends.

   • At the point or points in between—where the figure variation is greatest, changes from an even to an uneven amount, or begins to taper into the original seamline. The greater the curve, the more pivot points may be needed to maintain a smooth seamline.

   • At the base of darts affected by the alteration, on one or both sides of the dart, depending on the variation.

11. Draw a line across the seam allowance at each pivot point. (See step B.)

12. Cut the affected seam allowance free from the pattern, cutting just inside the seamline. Larger scissors indicate where to begin cutting. Cut carefully. (See step C.)

13. Clip the lines drawn across the seam allowance. Clip to, but not through, the pivot point on the seamline. This creates a sort of "hinge" that allows you to move the seam allowance in or out, and enables the seam allowance to lie flat. Smaller scissors indicate where to clip. Clip carefully. (See step D.)

14. Tape the unaffected pattern edges to the alteration paper underneath.

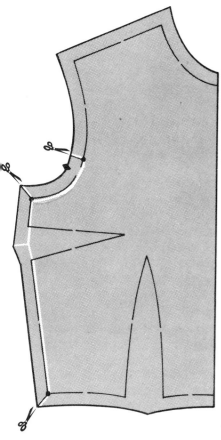

D Clip the lines drawn across the seam allowances at each pivot point. Do not cut through the seam stitching line.

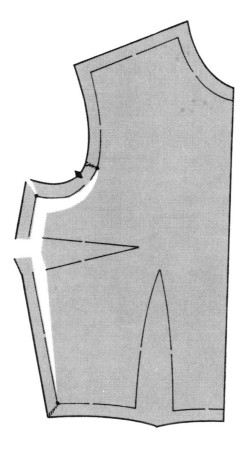

E Slide the free ends of the seam allowance away from the pattern to increase width an uneven amount and to increase dart size.

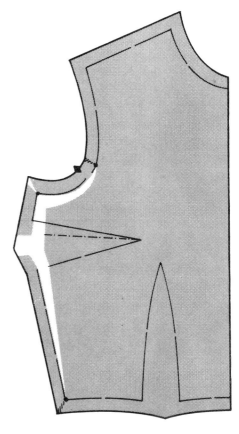

F Restore dart stitching lines, cutting lines, and seam stitching lines.

15. Slide or pivot the free seam allowance in the required direction and amount. Open or white space indicates an increase in size. Diagonal lines indicate a decrease in size. (See step E.)

- Slide the entire free seam allowance away from the pattern to increase length or width an even amount (spread).

- Slide the entire free seam allowance onto the pattern to decrease length or width an even amount (overlap).

- Slide/pivot the free end of the seam allowance away from the pattern to increase length or width an uneven amount (spread).

- Slide/pivot the free end of the seam allowance onto the pattern to decrease length or width an uneven amount (overlap).

- Slide then pivot the free seam allowance away from or onto the pattern to alter for both even and uneven amounts.

When you make an uneven amount of change in length that involves the center front or center back, you must begin with an even amount of change for a distance of about 2 to 4 inches from the center. This insures a right angle at the center front or center back so that seamlines intersect correctly. This distance often coincides conveniently with a dart. You can then taper or blend the remaining distance into the original seamline.

16. Tape the altered seam allowance securely in place.

17. Restore dart seamlines, cutting lines, seamlines, notches, marks and symbols disturbed by the alteration. Use an appropriate ruler to aid you in blending any lines. (See step F.)

FIGURE 5.2
EXAMPLES OF THE SEAM METHOD FOR NARROW HIPS.

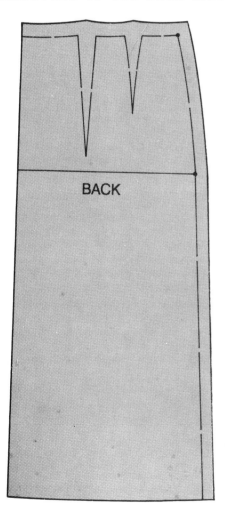

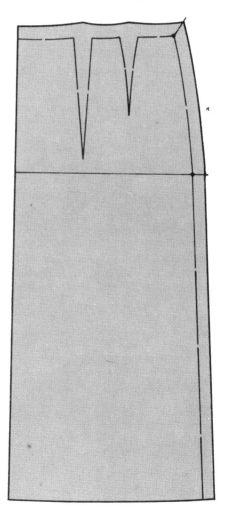

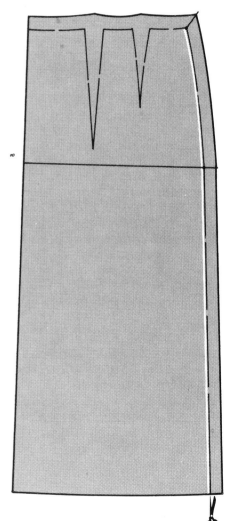

A Mark pivot points.

B Draw a line across the seam allowance at each pivot point.

C Cut the affected seam allowance free from the pattern, just inside the stitching line.

- Use a ruler and/or French curve to draw straight and curved lines accurately.

- If you are unsure about dart ends, fold the dart and turn it in the finished direction. Cut the dart base off according to the overlapping pattern cutting line. This will automatically restore the correct end shape.

18. Alter any pattern pieces that join an altered pattern piece so that seamlines match when sewn together—front, back, sleeve, collar, facing, etc.

19. Double check the accuracy of the alteration accordingly to the standards listed at the begining of the chapter.

20. Label the alteration on the pattern. Note the name of the figure variation and amount of change.

These examples illustrate step-by-step procedures, A through F, involved in the seam method of pattern alteration. Some detail is lost in the printed reduction of the originally altered pattern. On these examples only, a narrow white line identifies cutting and clip lines. If you want to test the altered pattern, pin-fit the pattern or sew a fitting garment in muslin or gingham.

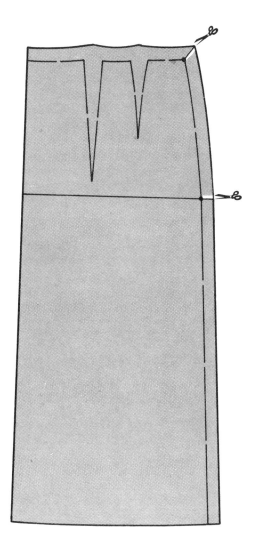

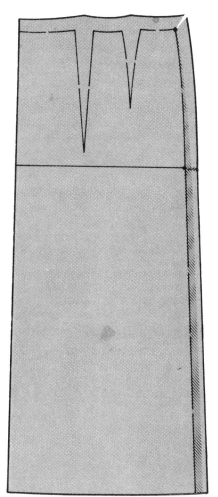

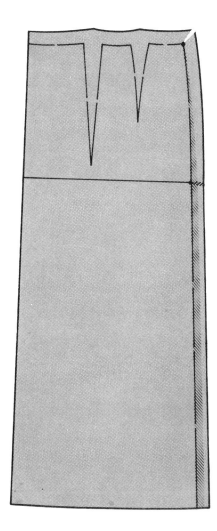

D Clip the lines drawn across the seam allowances at each pivot point. Do not cut through the seam stitching line.

E Slide the free end of the seam allowance onto the pattern to decrease width an uneven amount. Taper the overlap from waist to hip. Keep overlap parallel from hip to bottom of skirt.

F Lines at waist, hip level and bottom of skirt may need to be blended slightly.

Chapter 6
Figure Variations & Fitting Problems

This chapter is arranged in a format which illustrates and describes the following:

• Figure Variation
• Fitting Problem
• Fabric and Pattern Alteration
• Fashion Styles To Fit and Flatter

Under the heading *Figure Variation,* anatomical structures contributing to the variation are identified in terms of where they occur, how they may appear, and variation in size. For example, "The arm bones are longer than average. Increased length can occur in the upper arm, lower arm, or be distributed between both upper and lower arm."

Because figure variations seldom occur in isolation, other figure variations that often occur in combination with the variation are identified. For example, "Narrow hips can appear in combination with a high hip curve or below average weight." When applicable, the typical body type in which the variation commonly occurs is identified.

The section headed *Fitting Problem* identifies the fitting problem in terms of the fabric and how it appears on the body when ill-fitted. It provides a good base for comparison between body and garment.

The seamlines and hemlines in a basic garment pull and drop out of position when fitted with the least amount of ease. Wrinkles are clues to poor fit and can help you identify the figure variation and the fitting problem. Tight and loose wrinkles will form in a basic garment, exposing or leading attention to the figure variation causing the wrinkles.

Evaluate the fit of your own clothing, and the clothing of others, for evidence of the same or similar clues to poor fit. For example, "There is not enough fabric across the bust area. Fabric is pulled tight across the bust area. Horizontal wrinkles may form between the bust points. A buttoned closure may gap between the buttons."

Progressing from problem to solution, the section headed *Fabric and Pattern Alteration* provides you with instructions for the simplest method of alteration, generally the seam method. It begins with a general statement of garment need in terms of fabric length and/or width and shape, to fit the specific figure variation. For example, "The garment needs more fabric width to fit across wider shoulders."

Next, major steps required to execute the alteration are outlined, as simply and directly as possible. For example, "Shorten (take up) the garment evenly at the hem. The pattern can also be shortened evenly at approximately mid-upper and/or mid-lower arm, using the slash method as illustrated."

Study the accompanying illustration to help you visualize the printed words, but do not rely on the illustration alone. Thoroughly read all printed information accompanying each illustration. This information is critical to your initial understanding. Thereafter, you may rely on the illustrations to refresh your memory.

You can adapt the seam method for use on the paper pattern, finished garments, and garments during construction. On a practice pattern, carry out each alteration as outlined and illustrated. Compare your finished alteration to the illustration. Review basic alteration guidelines, found in Chapter 5.

Loose-fitting fashion garments may not expose the variation and require no alteration. Therefore, alteration instructions for garments of these types are not included. Multi-section fashion garments demand experience and advanced information on fitting and alteration. For additional information, see *Fitting and Pattern Alteration: A Multi-Method Approach* by Liechty, Pottberg and Rasband. All of the variations covered are cross-referenced to *Fitting and Pattern Alteration* at the end of this book.

Under the heading *Fashion Styles To Fit and Flatter* you will find a list of design details and fashion styles in classic clothes and accessories that, when well-fitted, you can expect to flatter your figure. The list is not intended to be exhaustive. You will discover that some figure variations don't need or even have as many fashion solutions to choose from as do others. The list is intended to include enough items to get you thinking in terms of styles that lead the eye in a desired direction, and camouflage or counter to create attractive illusions about the specific figure variation. Fashion illustrations represent only a few of the design details or garment styles listed.

Garment and accessory lists are arranged according to their approximate vertical position as worn on the body, starting from the head and moving downward. For example, styling details in the bodice area are listed first, followed by details in the waist, then hips, and so on down the body. Accessories might begin with reference to a hat, followed by a necklace, belt, and so on down the body, with shoes listed last. There may be minor exceptions, where reference to several design details, garments or accessories are included in one point of advice. Details and styles to generally avoid are also listed, followed by any special note of importance.

Bodices

This section covers selected figure variations occurring in the upper torso as well as fitting problems that result in the bodice area of a garment. Figure variations are arranged according to their approximate vertical position on the body, starting from the head and moving downward. For example, figure variations in the neck area are presented first, followed by variations in the shoulders, chest and upper back, bust, and so on.

Larger, Thick Neck

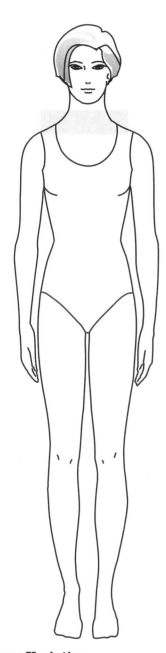

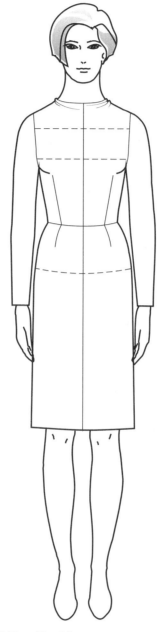

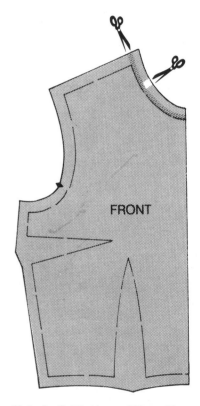

FRONT

Figure Variation
- The neck is larger or thicker than average/ideal. The back of the neck may not be noticeably affected.
- A larger, thicker neck can occur in combination with a generally more muscular body or above average/ideal weight.
- A larger, thicker neck can be shorter or appear to be shorter.

Fitting Problem
- In fitted necklines, there is too much fabric to fit comfortably around the base of the neck.
- The high, tight neckline cuts uncomfortably into the base of the neck.
- A circular wrinkle forms around the neck.
- Vertical pull lines can also form around the neck, at sides and front.
- The way the armhole fits may therefore be affected.

Fabric & Pattern Alteration
- The garment needs a larger opening—less fabric around the base of the larger neck.
- Lower and widen (enlarge) the neckline.
- If the back neckline does not need to be lowered, taper into the original seam at center back.
- Make the corresponding facing or collar larger in the neckline.

Fashions to Fit & Flatter

General Guidelines
- Camouflage, balance or draw attention down or away from a larger neck to create the illusion of a slimmer, longer neck.
- Necklines and collars that require little or no alteration lie or stand away from the neck. Collars open or unbuttoned at the neck seldom need alteration.

Design Details & Specific Styling
- V-, U-, and low rectangular necklines; slit, keyhole, sweetheart, and off-the-shoulder necklines; longer collar points, chelsea, shawl, and low-draped cowl collars; narrower, lower lapels; layer high-fitting necklines or collars with low-fitting necklines or collars.
- Cardigan jackets and sweaters worn open.
- Strapless or spaghetti-strap dresses.

Accessories
- Brimless, narrow brim or turned-up hats.
- Small to medium-sized earrings.
- Long or pendant necklaces. Scarves looped, knotted or bowed low on the chest.

Avoid
- Exposing or emphasizing a large or short neck with fussy, frilly necklines and collars; bulky or high-buttoned collars; high-tied or big bows; Victorian and turtleneck collars.
- Thick, heavy shoulder pads or epaulets.
- Droopy or broad-brimmed hats.
- Chunky earrings.
- Choker or "dog collar" necklace.
- Scarves worn wrapped or tied under the chin, a muffler or ascot.

Smaller, Thin Neck

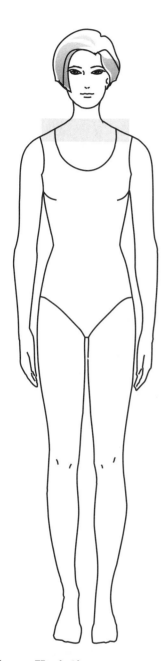

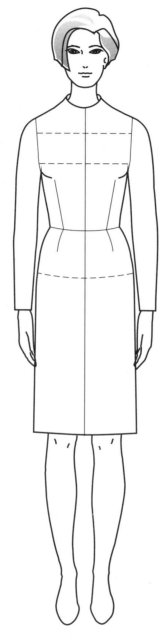

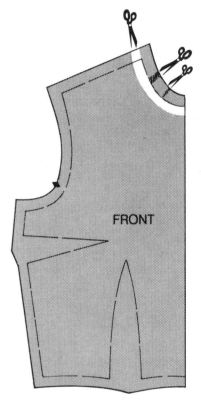

FRONT

Figure Variation

- The neck is smaller or thinner than average/ideal.
- A smaller, thinner neck can occur in combination with a generally less muscular body or below average/ideal weight.
- A smaller, thinner neck can be longer or appear to be longer.

Fitting Problem

- In fitted necklines, there is not enough fabric to fill in around the base of the neck.
- The low, loose fitting neckline gapes or stands unattractively away from the neck.

Fabric & Pattern Alteration

- The garment needs a smaller neck opening—more fabric around the base of the neck.
- Raise and narrow the neckline.
- On ready-to-wear garments, the shoulder seam can be taken in at the shoulder, or back neck darts can be added.
- Make corresponding facing or collar smaller in the neckline.

Fashions to Fit & Flatter

General Guidelines

- Camouflage, balance or draw attention out and away from a thin neck to create the illusion of a larger, shorter neck. Frame or fill in the neck area.
- Necklines and collars that require no alteration lie close but loose around the neck.

Design Details & Specific Styling

- Bateau, boatneck, wide V- and wide scoop necklines or collars; drawstring, bowed and ruffled necklines; funnel, mandarin, Victorian, high-draped cowl collars, loose-fitting turtleneck and other stand-up collars; medium to wide lapels.
- Epaulets

Accessories

- Broad-brimmed or droopy hats.
- Medium to larger earrings.
- Multiple chains, strands of beads or pearls.
- Scarves looped, knotted or bowed at the neck; an ascot, jabot or muffler.

Avoid

- Exposing or emphasizing a thin or long neck with plain necklines and extremely tight-fitting turtleneck collar.
- Unbroken vertical center front lines or closures.

Forward Neck (and Head)

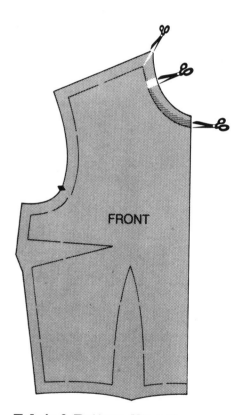

FRONT

Figure Variation
- The head and neck are thrust forward more than average/ideal.
- The angle where the neck joins the chest is sharper and essentially lower.
- The upper back area becomes longer.

Fitting Problem
- In fitted necklines, there is too much fabric in front and too little in back to fit attractively and comfortably.
- The high, tight neckline cuts uncomfortably into the front of the neck.
- A circular wrinkle forms around the neck base in front.
- Shoulder seamlines pull forward at the neck.
- The waistline may be pulled up at center back as the back neckline rises. (The center back may simply pull tight, held in place by a waistline seam.)

Fabric & Pattern Alteration
- The forward neck requires the garment front to be lowered, and the garment back to be raised, both to fit attractively and comfortably.
- Lower the front neckline and taper into the original shoulder seam.
- Raise the back shoulder seam at the neck and taper into the original seam at the armhole if needed.

Fashions to Fit & Flatter

General Guidelines
- Camouflage, balance, or draw attention down and away from a forward neck to create the illusion of a straighter neck.
- Open or loose-fitting necklines and collars require no alteration.

Design Details & Specific Styling
- Collars that fill in the angle in front of the neck, such as convertible notched, cowl, bowed and ruffled collars; layered necklines and collars.
- Gathers or released tucks in the front shoulder seamline.
- Interesting details at the waist or below.

Accessories
- Scarves that fill in the angle in front of the neck.

Avoid
- Exposing or emphasizing a forward neck with form fitting tops; jewel necklines—or alter them to fit comfortably.
- Long, dangling earrings.
- Long, heavy necklaces.
- Heavy or low-hanging scarves that appear to weigh you down in front.

Dowager Hump

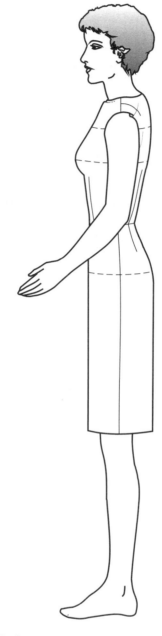

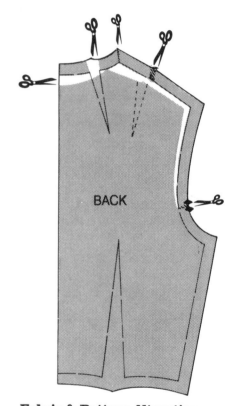

BACK

Figure Variation

- The upper back, at the base of the neck, curves outward more than average/ideal.
- The distance in length and width increases at the base of the neck.
- The curvature of the upper back, traditionally called the "dowager hump" often occurs in combination with a forward head and neck, and possibly a shallow chest.

Fitting Problem

- There is not enough fabric in the garment upper back.
- The garment pulls tight across the upper back.
- The waistline may be pulled up at center back as the back neckline rises. (The center back may simply pull tight, held in place by a waistline seam.)
- A circular wrinkle may form around the neckline in front.
- A horizontal ripple may form in the back armhole.

Fabric & Pattern Alteration

- The garment needs more fabric length and width to fit the upper back curvature attractively and comfortably.
- Lengthen (raise) the upper back area and taper into the original shoulder seam.
- Widen (let out) the upper back area and taper into the original armhole seam.
- Create back neck darts.

Fashions to Fit & Flatter

General Guidelines
- Camouflage, balance or draw attention away from the curvature to create the illusion of a straighter neck and upper back.
- Open or loose-fitting necklines and collars may require little or no alteration.

Design Details & Specific Styling
- Collars that stand away from or fill in the neck area, such as flat or partial roll collars; cowl, back-bowed and ruffled collars; layered necklines and collars.
- Gathers or released tucks in the back shoulder seamline; shirred shoulder yoke.
- Details at the waist or below.
- Loose-fitting tops.
- Textured fabrics.
- Small-scale, all-over pattern on fabric.

Accessories
- Scarves or shawls that fill in the area above and below the upper back.

Avoid
- Exposing or emphasizing the curvature with plain necklines; jewel necklines unless altered to fit comfortably; sailor collars.
- Drop shoulders and raglan sleeves.
- Back neck zipper.
- Low shoulder yoke.
- Strapless, sleeveless or form fitting tops.
- Clingy fabrics.
- Long, dangling earrings.
- Long, heavy necklaces.
- Scarves that appear to weigh you down in front.

Special Note: Medium to long hair styles, with soft fullness below the base of the neck, conceals a dowager hump.

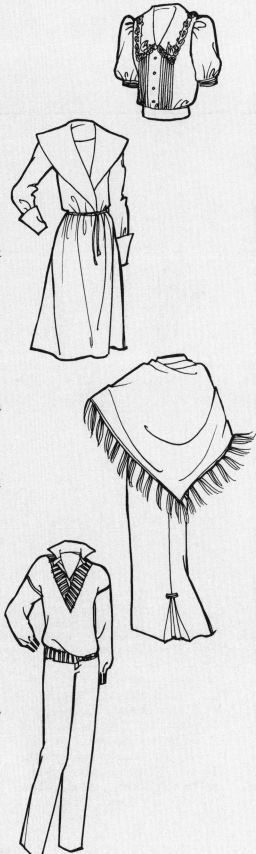

Wide (Broad) Shoulders

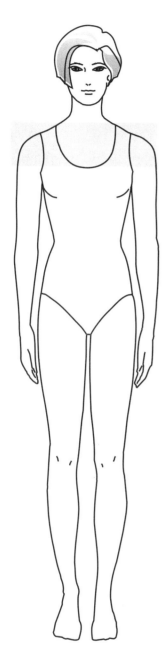

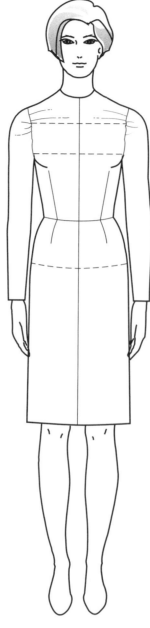

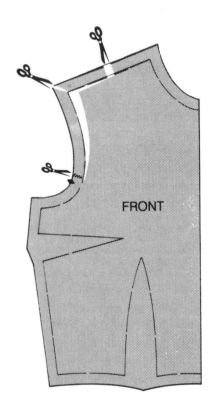

FRONT

Figure Variation
- Wide (Broad) Shoulders
- The shoulder or collar bones are longer than average/ideal.
- The entire bone structure can be larger than average.
- Wider shoulders are characteristic of an inverted triangle body type.
- Shoulders can actually be average but appear wider in proportion to a narrow midriff, waist or narrow hips.

Fitting Problem
- There is not enough fabric width to fit across the shoulders.
- Fabric is tight across the upper chest, shoulder and upper sleeve.
- The armhole seamline is pulled.
- Tight horizontal wrinkles or ripples may form across the chest and around the sleeve cap.
- Short, tight, wrinkles may radiate from the armhole seamline.

Fabric & Pattern Alteration
- The garment needs more fabric width to fit across wider shoulders.
- Lengthen (let out) the shoulder seamline and taper into the original seam at the underarm.

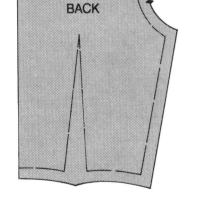

Fashions to Fit & Flatter

General Guidelines
- Camouflage, balance or draw attention inward and away from wide shoulders to create the illusion of narrower shoulders.
- Clothes that require little or no alteration include full upper sleeves, oversized tops, jackets and coats.

Design Details & Specific Styling
- Narrow V- and U-shaped necklines, a Henley neckline, a funnel neckline; notched collars worn open, a low-draped cowl, mandarin, shawl, softly bowed or stock tie collar; narrow lapels.
- Epaulets on shoulders, with buttoned tabs that point toward the neck.
- Sleeves set 1/4" to 1/2" inside natural seamline, and gathered or puff sleeves set 1" inside natural seamline; shirt style, drop-shoulder, kimono, raglan, dolman and batwing sleeves; sleeves flared at the wrist.
- Pockets at the hip.
- Blouson and tunic tops.
- Unconstructed and cardigan jackets.
- Flared, softly gathered, and unpressed-pleat skirts.
- Caftans, princess, tent, and trapeze dresses.
- Pleat-front pants.
- Flared coats and capes.
- Softer fabrics in flat to medium textures.

Accessories
- Wide-brimmed hats.
- Jabot
- A pin at center front.
- Longer necklaces.

Avoid
- Emphasizing broad shoulders with bateau, wide square or shallow scoop and off-the-shoulder necklines; boatneck, sailor, puritan, portrait, or ruffle collars; wide or peaked lapels.
- Sleeveless, cap, cape and butterfly sleeves; large or bulky shoulder pads.
- Fussy, frilly tops.
- Pegged or tapered skirts and pants.
- Horizontal and chevron stripes.
- Clingy, stiff, or thick and heavy fabric in the shoulder area.
- Small hats.
- Tight, wide belts.
- Small handbags.

Special Note: Broad shoulders can be a fashion asset to balance or visually narrow the hips or thighs, and to increase visual presence. If you choose to make broad shoulders part of your personal style, then make the most of them and enjoy!

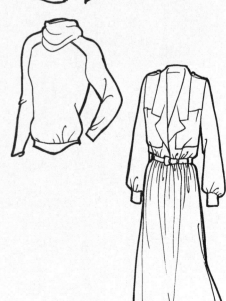

Narrow Shoulders

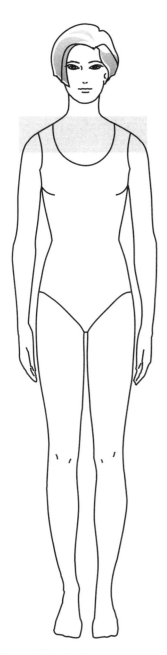
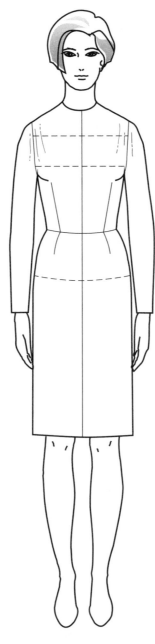
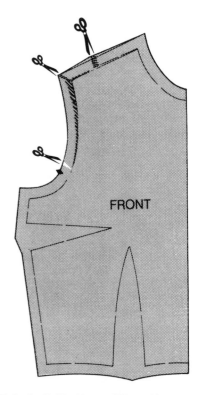

Figure Variation

- The shoulder or collar bones are shorter than average/ideal.
- The entire bone structure can be smaller than average.
- Narrower shoulders are characteristic of a triangular and a diamond-shaped body type.
- Shoulders can actually be average but appear narrower in proportion to a wider midriff, waist or wide hips.

Fitting Problem

- There is too much fabric width across the shoulders.
- Fabric is loose across the upper chest, shoulder and upper sleeve.
- The armhole seamline falls off the curved end of the shoulder.
- Loose vertical wrinkles or ripples form at the sides of the chest and on the sagging sleeve cap.

Fabric & Pattern Alteration

- The garment needs less fabric width to fit narrower shoulders.
- Shorten (take in) the shoulder seamline and taper into the original seam at the underarm.

Fashions to Fit & Flatter

General Guidelines
- Camouflage, balance or draw attention outward and away from narrow shoulders to create the illusion of wider shoulders.
- Clothes that require little or no alteration feature softly styled, loose-fitting sleeves designed without a shoulder seam—but usually demand a shoulder pad.

Design Details & Specific Styling
- Bateau, sabrina, sweetheart, off-the-shoulder, and wide scoop necklines; smaller notched collars, wing, boatneck, sailor, bertha, portrait, and wide cowl collars; medium and peaked lapels.
- Button shoulders; epaulet with buttoned tabs pointing toward the shoulder and tabs around the shoulders; shoulder pads.
- Sleeves set 1/2" outside the natural seamline; cap, cape, butterfly, pleated, puffed, mellon and leg-o-mutton sleeves.
- Gathers, tucks and pleats in the shoulder seam or yokeline.
- Breast pockets.
- Double-breasted closures.
- Loose-fitting, bloused or full-belted bodice.
- Sweater sets.
- Pinafore.
- Narrow, soft or straight hanging skirts and slacks; flared if hops or thighs are wide.
- Boxy jackets and coats.
- Layered looks.
- Medium to bulky fabrics in shoulder area.
- Horizontal and wide chevron stripes in shoulder area.

Accessories
- Narrow-brim hats.
- Shawls.

Avoid
- Emphasizing narrow shoulders with lines or details that draw attention inward, including a bold vertical center line.
- Narrow V- and U-shaped necklines, keyhole and drawstring necklines; wide or long collar points; low-draped cowl collars; narrow lapels.
- Raglan and tight-fitted long sleeves; bulky sleeve cuffs.
- Princess, tent and trapeze dresses.
- Wide flare and bouffant skirts.
- Full, harem pants.
- Clingy, limp or very heavy fabrics.
- Wide-brimmed hats.

Square Shoulders

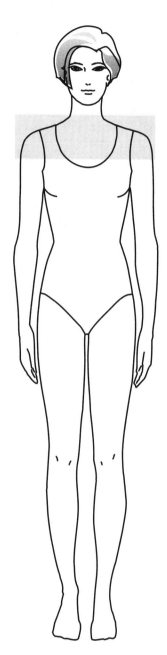

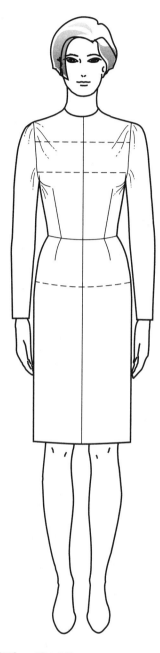

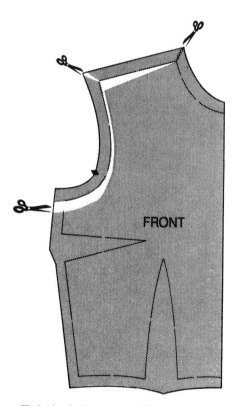

FRONT

Figure Variation
- The shoulder or collar bones slant downward less than average/ideal. They appear high at the ends.
- Distance increases between the waist and underarm.
- Do not confuse square shoulders with a shallow neck base at sides.
- Square shoulders can occur in combination with an overly erect upper back.

Fitting Problem
- There is not enough fabric length at the underarm.
- As fabric pulls tight, diagonal wrinkles form between the bust or blade and shoulder—angled toward the shoulder.
- Sleeves may be pulled up and appear too short.

Fabric & Pattern Alteration
- The garment needs the armhole raised to decrease shoulder slant for square shoulders.
- Lengthen (raise) the bodice side seam at the underarm and raise the corresponding shoulder seam.

Fashions to Fit & Flatter

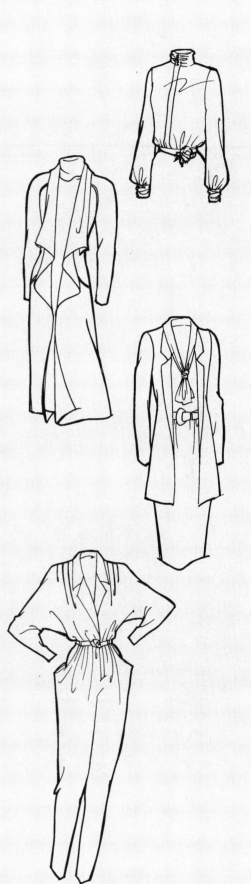

General Guidelines
- Camouflage, balance or draw attention inward and down from square shoulders to create the illusion of less squared shoulders.
- Clothes that require little or no alteration include full upper sleeves, oversized tops, jackets and coats.

Design Details & Specific Styling
- Narrow V- and U-shaped necklines; built-up necklines; collars, such as a funnel, mandarin, softly bowed or stock tie and soft turtleneck collar; notched collars with longer collar points, worn open; narrow to medium lapels pointed down.
- Flat-lying epaulets with buttoned tabs that point toward the neck.
- Shirt style, drop-shoulder, kimono, raglan, dolman and batwing sleeves.
- Soft gathers, tucks or pleats at the shoulder yokeline.
- Blouson and tunic tops.
- Hip pockets and other details in skirt or pants.
- Softly unconstructed and cardigan jackets and coats.
- Softer fabrics in flat to medium textures; firmer, heavier fabrics in skirts and slacks.

Accessories
- Hats with down-sloping brim.
- Longer necklaces,
- A pin at center front.

Avoid
- Emphasizing square shoulders with lines that draw attention up, such as with a bateau, wide square or scoop necklines; boatneck, sailor, puritan or ruffle collars; wide or peaked lapels.
- Shoulder pads; sleeveless and cap sleeves.
- Fussy, frilly tops.
- Pegged or tapered skirts and pants.
- Clingy, stiff, or thick and heavy fabric in the shoulder area.
- Horizontal and chevron stripes in the shoulder area.
- Small hats.
- Tight, wide belts.
- Small, delicate handbags.

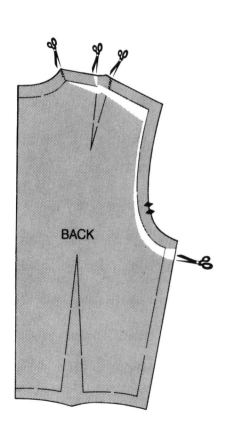

BACK

Sloped Shoulders

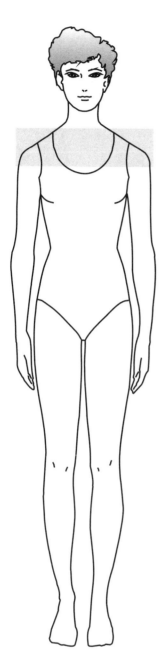

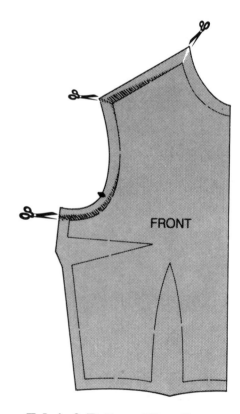

FRONT

Figure Variation

- The shoulder or collar bones slant downward more than average/ideal. They appear low at the ends.
- Distance decreases between the waist and underarm.
- Do not confuse square shoulders with a high neck base at sides.
- Sloped shoulders can occur in combination with rounded shoulders or a rounded upper back.

Fitting Problem

- There is too much fabric length at the underarm.
- As fabric sags, loose diagonal wrinkles or ripples form between the neck and underarm. Loose, sagging folds may appear at the underarm only.

Fabric & Pattern Alteration

- The garment needs the armhole lowered to increase shoulder slant for sloped shoulders.
- Shorten (lower) the bodice side seam at the underarm and lower the corresponding shoulder seam.

Fashions to Fit & Flatter

General Guidelines
- Camouflage, balance or draw attention upward or away from sloped shoulders to create the illusion of raised shoulders.
- Clothes that require little or no alteration feature loose fit and demand a shoulder pad.

Design Details & Specific Styling
- Bateau, sweetheart, and wide scoop necklines; narrow collar points, wing, boatneck, sailor, bertha, portrait, wide cowl and ruffle collars; medium and peaked lapels.
- Button shoulders, and epaulet with buttoned tab pointing toward the shoulder; shoulder pads.
- Set-in sleeves, cap, cape, butterfly, puffed, pleated, and leg-o-mutton sleeves.
- Breast pockets.
- Double-breasted closures.
- Loose-fitting, bloused or full-belted bodice.
- Sweater sets.
- Pinafore.
- Narrow, soft or straight hanging skirts and slacks.
- Boxy jackets and coats.
- Layered looks.
- Medium to bulky fabrics.
- Chevron stripes in shoulder area; details in the waist area.

Accessories
- Hats with an up-turned brim.
- Shawls.

Avoid
- Exposing or emphasizing sloped shoulders with lines or details that draw attention inward or downward, such as strapless, narrow V- and U-shaped necklines, keyhole, halter, drawstring and off-the-shoulder necklines; funnel, Victorian, or turtleneck collars and low-draped bow or cowl collar; narrow and wide lapels, lapels that point down.
- A saddle yoke.
- Drop-shoulder, kimono, raglan, cape and flared sleeves or tight-fitted long sleeves; bulky sleeve cuffs.
- Wide-flare and bouffant skirts.
- Princess, tent and trapeze dresses.
- Baggy or harem pants.
- Clingy, limp, or very heavy fabrics.
- Vertical and downward diagonal stripes; horizontal stripes or border print in the shoulder area.
- Droopy brimmed hats.
- Heavy necklace or pendant.

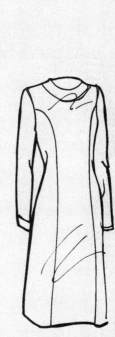

BACK

Rounded Chest

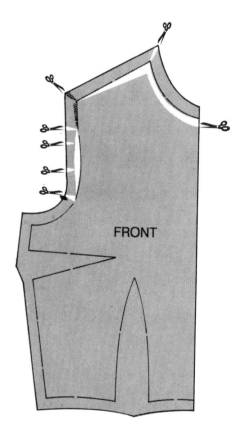

FRONT

Figure Variation
- The sternum protrudes more than average/ideal.
- The chest rounds out more than average/ideal, just below the neck.
- Distance increases over and across the upper chest.

Fitting Problem
- There is not enough fabric length and width to fit across the upper chest.
- The edges of a garment opening do not meet.
- If forced to meet and fasten, or if one piece, fabric pulls tight across the chest.
- Diagonal wrinkles may form between the neckline and armhole.

Fabric & Pattern Alteration
- The garment needs more fabric length and width to fit the rounded chest.
- Lengthen (raise) the garment neckline at center front, tapering into original waistline at the armhole.
- Widen (let out) the garment at the armhole.

Fashions to Fit & Flatter

General Guidelines
- Camouflage or draw attention away from a rounded chest to create the illusion of a flatter chest. Fill in areas above and below the chest.
- Clothes that require little or no alteration feature a loose fit in the bodice front.

Design Details & Specific Styling
- Convertible notch collars worn open; a high bowed, stock tie, or cowl collar; low-set lapels.
- Epaulets on shoulders; wide-set shoulder straps.
- Gathers, tucks or soft pleats from the shoulder seamline.
- Tops bloused in the midriff and waist.
- Unbuttoned vests, sweaters and jackets.
- Trench coat.
- Layered looks.
- All-over patterns on fabric.

Accessories
- Hats.
- Earrings.
- Pin at the throat.
- Short necklaces.
- Scarf at the neck.

Avoid
- Exposing a rounded chest with low necklines; keyhole, halter, bandeau, strapless necklines; turtleneck, Victorian, collars
- Sleeveless tops; puffy sleeves
- Large buttons down the front.
- Clingy, form-fitting fabrics or knits.
- Horizontal stripes or border print across the chest.
- Man-style ties, necklaces and pins on the mid-chest area.

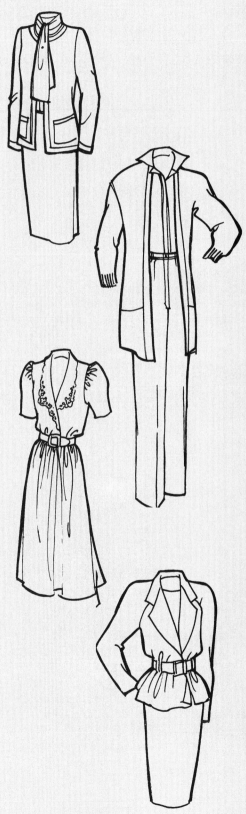

Shallow Chest

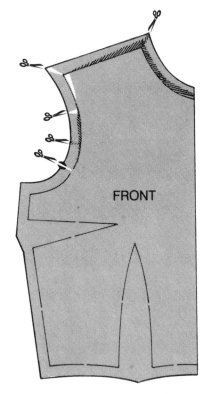

FRONT

Figure Variation
- The chest is flatter than average/ideal.
- There is no chest curve below the neck.
- Distance decreases over and across the upper chest
- Shallow chest can occur in combination with a ronded upper back and shoulders.

Fitting Problem
- There is too much fabric length and width over the upper chest.
- The garment hangs loose or sags in the upper chest area, above the bust.
- Horizontal folds or ripples may form.

Fabric & Pattern Alteration
- The garment needs less fabric length and width to flatter a shallow upper chest.
- Shorten (lower) the garment neckline at center front, tapering into original waistline at the armhole.
- Decrease (take in) garment width at the armhole.

Fashions to Fit & Flatter

General Guidelines
- Camouflage, fill in or draw attention away from a shallow chest to create the illusion of a fuller chest.
- Clothes that require little or no alteration feature soft fullness in the chest area.

Design Details & Specific Styling
- Notched collars; cowl, bowed, stock tie, and ruffled collars.
- Gathers, smocking, shirring, released tucks or pleats in the front shoulder seamline or yokeline.
- High-set breast pockets.
- Vests, sweaters and sweater sets.
- Layered looks.
- Textured fabric in the chest area.

Accessories
- Earrings.
- Chest-length necklaces; multiple necklaces.
- Pins on the chest.
- Scarves that fill in the front of the neck.

Avoid
- Exposing a shallow chest with plain, flat or low necklines; keyhole and slit necklines.
- Form-fitting tops.
- Clingy, form-fitting fabrics or knits.
- Long, dangling earrings.
- Long, heavy necklaces.
- Scarves tied low.

Special Note: Many neckline and bodice details that cover and camouflage a rounded chest also fill in a shallow chest.

Rounded Upper Back

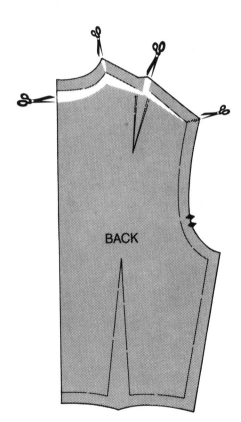

BACK

Figure Variation
- The entire upper back curves outward more than average/ideal.
- Distance increases between the neck and mid-back.
- A rounded upper back often occurs in combination with rounded shoulders and/or a shallow chest.

Fitting Problem
- There is not enough fabric length or curved shaping in the upper back area.
- The garment pulls tight in the upper back area.
- Diagonal wrinkles may form between the neck and armhole.
- The neckline may be pulled tightly down in back and up in front.
- The waistline may be pulled up at center back.

Fabric & Pattern Alteration
- The garment needs more fabric length and shaping to fit a rounded upper back.
- Lengthen (raise) the upper back area and taper into original seam at the armhole.
- Widen the back shoulder darts.

Fashions to Fit & Flatter

General Guidelines
- Camouflage, balance or draw attention away from the rounded upper back curvature to create the illusion of a straighter back.
- Clothes that require little or no alteration feature a loose fit across the back and an open neckline in front.

Design Details & Specific Styling
- Flat or partial roll collars that stand away from or fill in the area below the neck; cowl, back-bowed and ruffled collars, layered necklines and collars.
- Shoulder pads.
- Gathers or released tucks in the back shoulder seamline; shirred shoulder yoke.
- Set-in sleeves; pleated or puffed sleeve cap.
- Details at the waist or below.
- Loose-fitting and bloused tops.
- Boxy jackets.
- Textured fabrics.
- Small-scale, all-over patterned fabrics.

Accessories
- Scarves or shawls that cover or fill in above the upper back.

Avoid
- Exposing or emphasizing a rounded upper back with form fitting tops.
- Low back and strapless necklines; jewel necklines or alter them to fit comfortably; sailor collars.
- Back neck zipper.
- Sleeveless tops; drop shoulder-sleeves, cape, and raglan sleeves.
- Princess seam lines.
- Peasant blouse.
- Thin, limp, clingy fabrics.
- Hats with a droopy brim.
- Long, dangling earrings.
- Long, heavy necklaces.
- Scarves that appear to weigh you down in front.

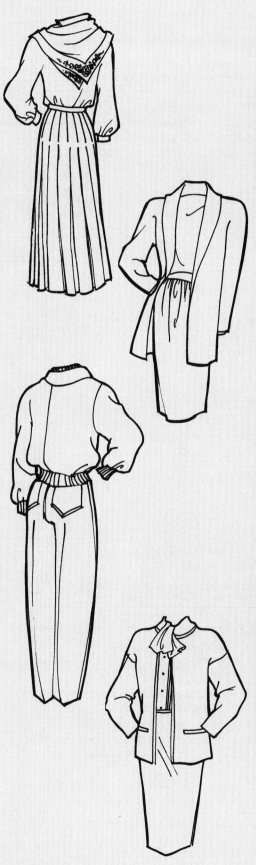

Erect Upper Back

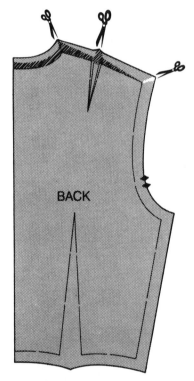

BACK

Figure Variation
- The entire upper back curves less than average/ideal.
- Distance decreases between the neck and mid-back.
- An erect back can occur in combination with square shoulders and/or a prominent bust.

Fitting Problem
- There is too much fabric length and curved shaping in the upper back area. The garment shaping or fullness sags in the upper back.
- Horizontal ripples may form across the upper back.
- The waistline may sag at center back.

Fabric & Pattern Alteration
- The garment needs less fabric length and curved shaping to fit an erect upper back.
- Shorten (lower) the upper back area and taper into original seamline at the armhole.
- Make the back shoulder darts narrower.

Fashions to Fit & Flatter

General Guidelines
- Camouflage, fill in or draw attention away from an overly erect back to create the illusion of a more natural back.

Design Details & Specific Styling
- Back-bowed or low-draped cowl neckline or collar.
- Gathers, tucks and pleats in the shoulder seam or yokeline.
- Loose-fitting, bloused or full-belted tops.
- Aviator, wrap or anorak jacket.
- Poncho, cape or trench coat with capelet
- Layered looks.
- Medium to bulky textured fabrics.

Accessories
- Shawl or stole to fill in both areas.

Avoid
- Exposing or emphasizing an overly erect back with form-fitting clothes.
- Large or bulky shoulder pads
- Clingy fabrics.

Special Note: If also present, avoid exposing a prominent bust.

Wide Chest/Upper Back

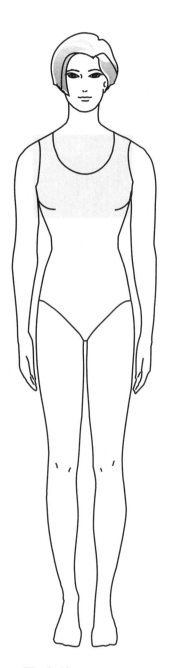

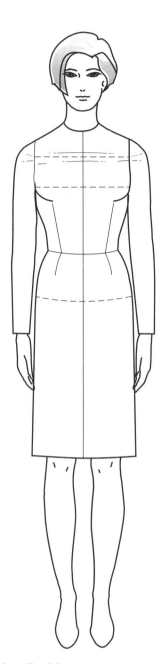

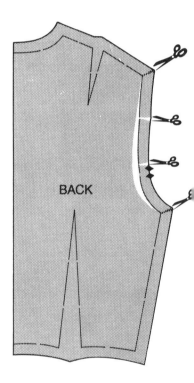

BACK

Figure Variation
- The chest and/or upper back is wider than average/ideal.
- A wide chest and/or upper back can occur in combination with wide shoulders and with above average/ideal weight.
- Increased width can extend lower, to the midriff area.

Fitting Problem
- There is not enough fabric width across the chest and/or upper back.
- The garment pulls tight across the chest and/or upper back.
- Tight horizontal wrinkles may form across the chest and/or upper back.
- Sleeve seamlines may be pulled inward, toward the chest or back.

Fabric & Pattern Alteration
- The garment needs more fabric width to fit a broad chest and/or upper back.
- Widen (let out) the chest and/or upper back in the armhole area.
- Extend alteration down into mid-back if needed.

Fashions to Fit & Flatter

General Guidelines
- Camouflage, balance or draw attention inward and away from a wide chest or back to create the illusion of narrower chest or back.
- Clothes that require little or no alteration include loose-fitting or oversized tops, jackets and coats.

Design Details & Specific Styling
- Narrow V- and U-shaped necklines, a henley neckline, a funnel neckline, man-styled notched collars worn open; a low-draped cowl, mandarin, shawl, softly bowed or stock tie collar; a jabot; narrow lapels.
- Epaulets on shoulders, with buttoned tabs that point toward the neck.
- Sleeves set 1/4" to 1/2" inside natural seamline; sleeveless tops; shirt style, drop-shoulder, kimono, raglan, dolman and batwing sleeves; sleeves flared at the wrist.
- Pockets at the hip.
- Blouson and tunic tops.
- Unconstructed and cardigan jackets.
- Caftans, princess, tent, and trapeze dresses.
- Flared skirts.
- Fuller, pleat-front pants.
- Flared coats and capes.
- Softer fabrics in flat to medium textures.

Accessories
- Wide-brimmed hats.
- A pin at center front.
- Longer necklaces.

Avoid
- Exposing or emphasizing a wide chest or upper back with a bateau, wide square, shallow scoop, or off-the-shoulder necklines; boatneck, sailor, puritan, portrait, or ruffle collars; wide or peaked lapels.
- Cap, cape puff, melon, butterfly, and leg-o-mutton sleeves; large or bulky shoulder pads; spaghetti straps.
- Fussy, frilly tops.
- Pegged or tapered skirts and pants.
- Form-fitting, clingy, stiff or thick and heavy fabrics.
- Horizontal and chevron stripes in chest or back area.
- Small hats.
- Tight, wide belts.
- Small handbags.

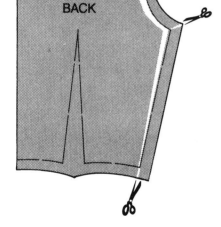

Narrow Chest/Upper Back

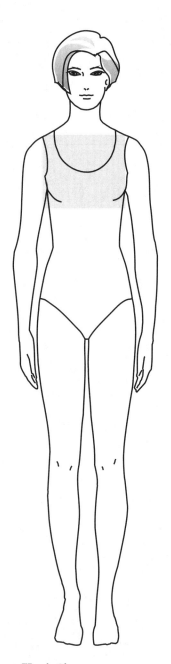

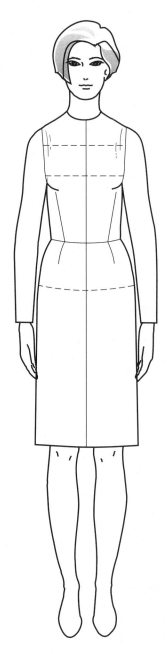

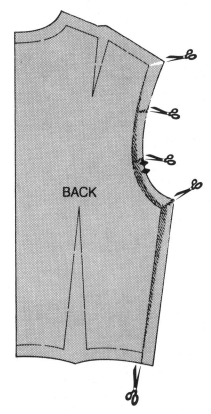

Figure Variation
- The chest and/or upper back is narrower than average/ideal.
- A narrow chest and/or upper back can occur in combination with narrow shoulders, an erect upper back, or below average/ideal weight.
- Decreased width can extend lower, to the midriff area.

Fitting Problem
- There is too much fabric width across the chest and/or upper back.
- The garment is loose across the chest and/or upper back.
- Loose vertical ripples may form, usually at the sides of the chest or upper back, near the armhole seamline.

Fabric & Pattern Alteration
- The garment needs less fabric width to fit a narrow chest and/or upper back.
- Narrow (take in) the chest and/or upper back in the armhole area.

Fashions to Fit & Flatter

General Guidelines
- Camouflage, balance or draw attention outward from a narrow chest or back to create the illusion of wider chest or back.
- Clothes that require little or no alteration feature a soft, loose fit.

Design Details & Specific Styling
- Bateau, sabrina, sweetheart, off-the-shoulder, and wide scoop necklines; smaller notched collars, wing, boatneck, sailor, bertha, portrait, and wide cowl collars; medium and peaked lapels.
- Button shoulders; epaulets with buttoned tabs pointing toward the shoulder; narrow shoulder straps; shoulder pads.
- Sleeves set 1/2" outside the natural seamline; cap, cape, butterfly, puffed, melon, and leg-o-mutton sleeves.
- Gathers, tucks and pleats in the shoulder seam or yokeline.
- Breast pockets.
- Double-breasted closures.
- Loose-fitting, bloused or full-belted tops.
- Sweater sets.
- Pinafore.
- Narrow, soft or straight hanging skirts and slacks.
- Boxy jackets and coats.
- Medium to bulky fabrics.
- Horizontal and wide vertical or chevron stripes.

Accessories
- Narrow-brim hats.
- Shawls

Avoid
- Exposing or emphasizing a narrow chest or upper back with narrow V- and U-shaped necklines, keyhole and drawstring necklines; wide or long collar points; low-draped cowl collars; narrow lapels.
- Raglan and tight-fitted long sleeves; bulky sleeve cuffs.
- Bold vertical center line.
- Large buttons.
- Sleeveless and halter tops.
- Wide-flare and bouffant skirts.
- Princess, tent and trapeze dresses.
- Full, harem pants.
- Clingy, limp or very heavy fabrics.
- Wide-brimmed hats.

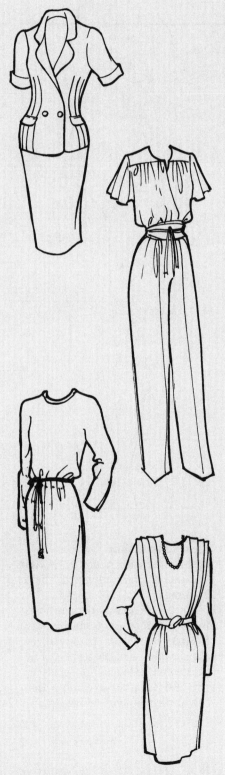

Larger Bust

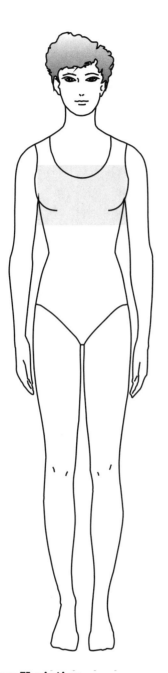

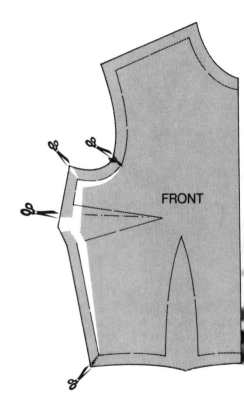

FRONT

Figure Variation

- The breasts, or bust, are larger than average/ideal, assuming a "B" bra cup as average.
- Distance increases across the bust area. (In some cases, length is affected.)
- A larger bust is characteristic of an inverted triangle and hourglass body type, and can occur in combination with above average/ideal weight.

Fitting Problem

- There is not enough fabric width across the bust area.
- Fabric is tight across the bust area.
- Horizontal wrinkles may form between the bust tips, and a buttoned closure will gap between buttons.
- Diagonal wrinkles or ripples may form between the armhole and bust tip.
- The bodice side seam is pulled or bows forward, positioning the underarm dart near or over the bust tip.
- If length is affected, the waist and hemline are pulled up in front.

Fabric & Pattern Alteration

- The garment needs more fabric width and more curved shaping to fit a larger bust.
- Widen (let out) the bodice side seams at bust level.
- Widen underarm darts to fit the larger curve. Widen waist dart also if needed.
- If additional length is also needed, lengthen the pattern an even amount at bust level by slash method, or at waist level by seam method.
- Lower dart position if needed.

Fashions to Fit & Flatter

General Guidelines
- Camouflage, balance or draw attention up and away from a larger bust to create the illusion of a smaller bust.
- Clothes that require little or no alteration feature a loose fit from the shoulders or a shoulder yoke and are designed without bust-fitting darts in the side seam.

Design Details & Specific Styling
- Tailored style or convertible notch collars worn open at the neck; slit and shallow V-necklines; medium scale notched lapels.
- Medium-weight epaulets on shoulders.
- Set-in sleeves at three-quarter or wrist length; cuffs at the wrist; moderate shoulder pads.
- Small to medium button at the bustline.
- Dropped waistlines; narrow to medium waistbands.
- Slot, slash and in-seam pockets.
- Loose-fitting tops and dresses with released tucks or pleats controlled at the shoulder; caftans.
- Tunics and longer vests, cardigan sweaters and jackets, worn open.
- Flared, gored and stitched-down pleat skirts slightly longer.
- Straight, pleat-front pants, uncuffed. Longer coat or cape.
- Lightweight layered looks.
- Flat to medium textured fabrics that hold their shape or drape beautifully.

Accessories
- Larger earrings.
- Scarves and necklaces that lie above or below the bustline.
- Narrow to medium belts.

Avoid
- Exposing or emphasizing a larger bust with low or frilly necklines.
- Puff or full upper sleeves; flared or ruffled cuff on short sleeves.
- Shirring or smocking over the bust; frilly ruffles down the front.
- Large buttons.
- Midriff yoke.

- Short bolero, aviator, boxy jackets; wide-set double-breasted jackets.
- Sheath and bouffant skirts or dresses; high-waist or pegged skirts and pants; cuffed pants.
- Stiff, heavy, bulky, or clingy fabrics.
- Large bold prints and horizontal stripes.
- Necklace or scarf at bust level.
- Wide or tight belts.

FRONT

Smaller Bust

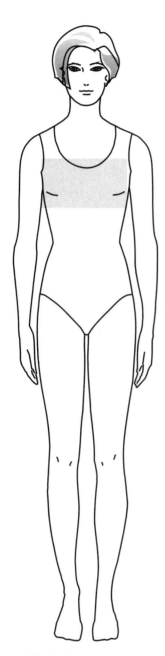

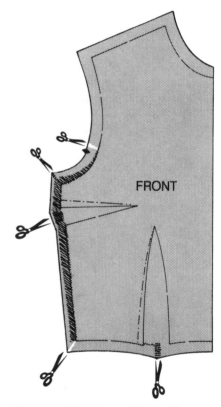

FRONT

Figure Variation

• The breasts, or bust, are smaller than average/ideal, assuming a "B" bra cup as average.

• Distance decreases across the bust area. (In some cases, length is affected.)

• A smaller bust is characteristic of a triangle and diamond-shaped body type, and can occur in combination with below average/ideal weight.

Fitting Problem

• There is too much fabric width across the bust area.

• Fabric is loose across the bust area.

• Loose vertical wrinkles or ripples may form across and/or at the sides of the bust.

• If length is affected, a loose horizontal fold may form underneath the bust.

• If length is affected, the waistline and hemline may sag in front.

Fabric & Pattern Alteration

• The garment needs less fabric width and less curved shaping to fit a smaller bust.

• Narrow (take in) the bodice side seams at bust level.

• Make underarm darts narrower to fit the smaller curve.

• Make waistline darts narrower as well, if needed.

• If length is also in excess, shorten the pattern an even amount at bust or waist level.

Fashions to Fit & Flatter

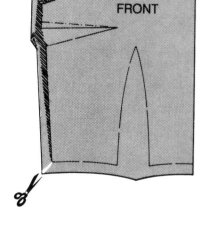

General Guidelines
- Camouflage, fill out, balance or draw attention away from a smaller bust to create the illusion of a larger bust.
- Clothes that require little or no alteration feature a loose, full fit in the bodice.
- Design Details & Specific Styling Boatneck, softly bowed, draped cowl, halter or ruffled neckline; rounded collars; a jabot; medium to wider notched lapels.
- Epaulets and shoulder yokes.
- Dropped-shoulder, puff, butterfly, cape, dolman, and leg-o-mutton sleeves; roll-up or long sleeves with cuffs; moderate shoulder pads.
- Gathers, shirring, smocking, tucks or pleats in the bodice.
- Breast pockets.
- Midriff yoke, empire and high-waistlines.
- Tops bloused at the waist.
- Short, shaped vests and sweaters; longer belted sweaters.
- Short, shapely jackets; bolero, aviator, safari, double-breasted and belted jackets.
- Straight, A-line, slightly flared, dirndl and flat-pleated skirts.
- Trench coats.
- Layered looks.
- Crisp, or thicker textured fabrics.
- Horizontal stripes, prints, plaids and buffalo checks.

Accessories
- Multi-strands of pearls or chain necklaces at bust level.
- Ascot or muffler; scarves at bust level.
- Wide or cinch belts.

Avoid
- Exposing or emphasizing a smaller bust with low, revealing necklines or collars.
- Sleeveless tops and bulky shoulder pads.
- Plain or extra-baggy tops; tight, form-fitting tops, dress bodices and sweaters.
- Sheer, flat or clingy fabrics.
- Vertical stripes.
- Heavy necklaces.

Special Note: If your hips, thighs or buttocks are proportionally larger, review those sections. Some of the styles that enhance a smaller bust may not enhance those figure variations, and therefore cancel some of the advice for a smaller bust, such as bolero jacket.

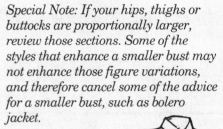

Longer Midriff/Low Waist

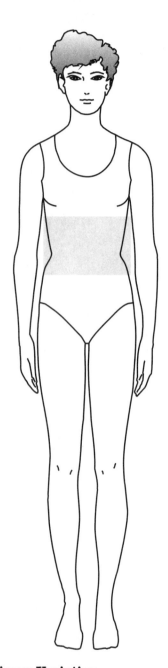

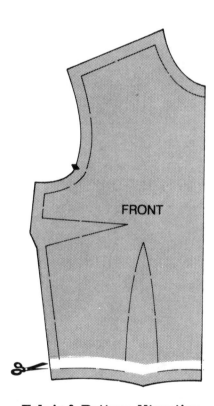

FRONT

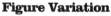

Figure Variation

- The distance between the bust and the waist is longer than average/ideal. (This variation is traditionally, yet inaccurately, called a "long waist.")
- A longer midriff can occur in combination with a shorter lower torso and/or shorter legs.

Fitting Problem

- There is not enough fabric length to cover the midriff.
- The garment waistline is positioned too high—above the body waistline.
- Tight horizontal wrinkles may form around the garment waistline.
- Underarm darts lie at mid-bust level, as they should.

Fabric & Pattern Alteration

- The garment needs more fabric length in the midriff—between the bust and the waist.
- Lengthen (lower) the midriff area by seam or slash method.

Fashions to Fit & Flatter

General Guidelines
- Camouflage, balance, or draw attention up and away from a long midriff to create the illusion of a shorter midriff.
- Clothes that require little or no alteration include separates and waistless designs.

Design Details & Specific Styling
- Wider necklines and collars.
- Shoulder yokes.
- 3/4 and roll up sleeves; full upper sleeves.
- Midriff yokes.
- Wider waistbands.
- "Blouse" tops above the waist or belt.
- Pullover vests and sweaters to high hip.
- Shorter jackets including aviator and safari styles.
- Belted sweaters and jackets.
- Waistless tops and dresses including shifts, chemise, A-line and princess line dresses; high-waisted skirts, dresses and pants, including empire styles.
- Flared, pleated or gathered skirts.
- Straight-leg and slim-cut pants.
- High-belted or straight-hanging coats.
- Layered looks.
- Bodice fabrics that hold their shape.
- Horizontal and diagonal lines in the midriff/waist area; vertical lines below the waist.

Accessories
- Wider belts and sashes; belts color matched to the skirt or pant; narrow belt of contrast color with short skirt or higher heel shoe.
- Mid to high heel shoes.

Avoid
- Exposing or emphasizing a long midriff with tight, form-fitting tops to the waist.
- Contrasting cuff on long sleeves.
- Fitted jackets.
- Short skirts.
- Waistless or low-waisted skirts and pants.
- Cropped or cuffed pants.
- Limp fabrics in the top; heavy fabrics in skirts and pants.
- Narrow vertical stripes above the waist.
- Wide belts color matched to the top.
- Heavy-textured stockings.
- Bulky flat shoes.

Special Note: If your legs are proportionally shorter, review that section. Some of the styles that flatter a longer midriff may not flatter shorter legs, and therefore cancel some of the above advice.

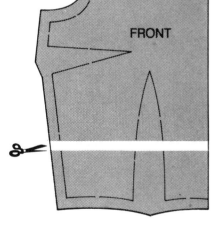

FRONT

Shorter Midriff/High Waist

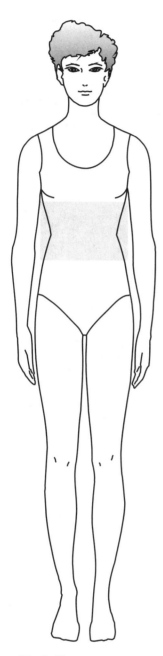

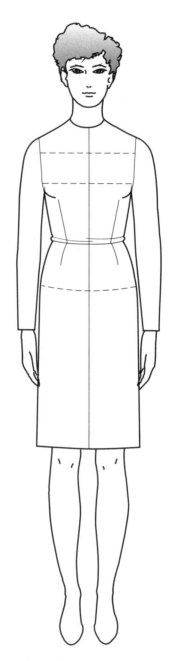

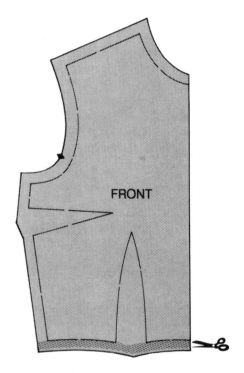

FRONT

Figure Variation

- The distance between the bust and the waist is shorter than average/ideal. (This variation is traditionally, yet inaccurately, called a "short waist.")
- A shorter midriff can occur in combination with a longer lower torso and/or longer legs.

Fitting Problem

- There is too much fabric length in the midriff.
- The garment waistline is positioned too low—below the body waistline.
- Loose horizontal folds may form around the garment waistline, resting on the hip bone.
- Underarm darts lie at mid-bust level, as they should.

Fabric & Pattern Alteration

- The garment needs less fabric length in the midriff—between the bust and the waist.
- Shorten (raise) the midriff area by seam or slash method.

Fashions to Fit & Flatter

General Guidelines
- Camouflage, balance, or draw attention away from a short midriff to create the illusion of a longer midriff.
- Clothes that require little or no alteration include separates and waistless designs.

Design Details & Specific Styling
- Stand-up, narrow necklines and collars.
- Shoulder pads and epaulets.
- Narrow waistbands.
- Shirts "bloused" to fold over the waistline; overblouses, blouson and tunic tops.
- Longer vests, sweaters and jackets to mid-hip or crotch-length.
- Waistless dresses including empire, A-line, shift, chemise and princess line dresses and jumpers; hip-wrap or coatdress; waistless, or drop waist skirts, dresses and pants.
- Flared or straight-hanging coats.
- Layered looks.
- Lighter-weight fabrics in bodice.
- Vertical and diagonal lines in the midriff/waist area; horizontal lines below the waist.

Accessories
- Contour and narrow to medium belts color matched to the top; narrow belt of contrast color with fuller skirt and lower heel shoe; low-riding belts.

Avoid
- Exposing or emphasizing a short midriff with form-fitting midriff area or midriff yoke; horizontal necklines and collars.
- Big, bulky sleeves.
- Eye-catching waistline details; wide waistband.
- Short vests, sweaters and jackets; fitted jackets.
- High-waisted skirts or pants.
- Box pleat or bulky skirts.
- Stiff or heavy fabrics above the waist.
- Horizontal stripes above the waist.
- Wider belt, cummerbund or sash; belts color matched to skirt or pants.

Special Note: If your legs are proportionally too long, review that section. Some of the styles that flatter a shorter midriff may not flatter noticeably long legs, and therefore cancel some of the above advice.

FRONT

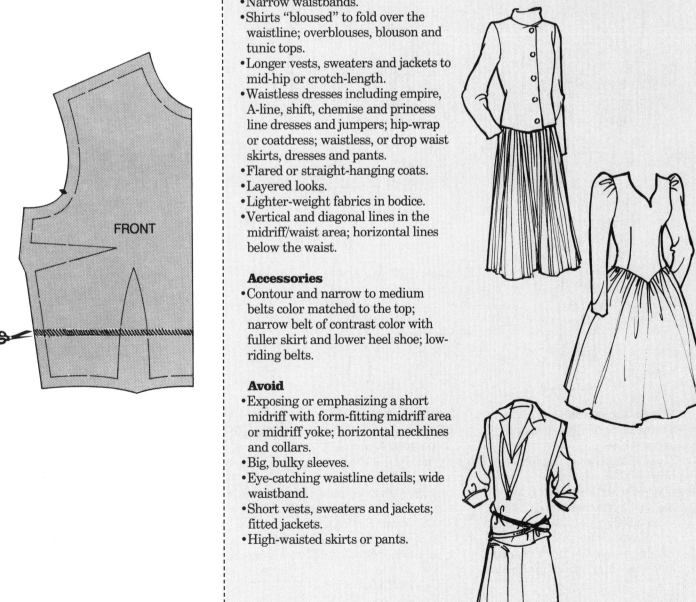

Larger Waist

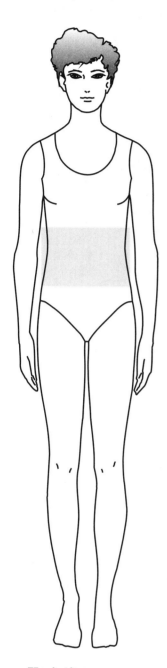

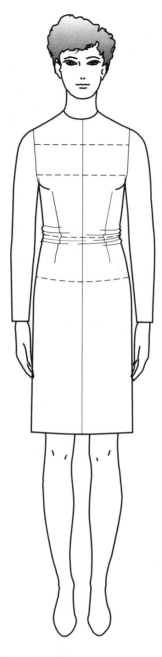

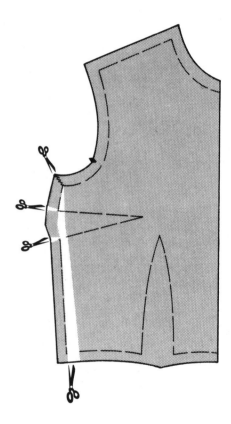

Figure Variation
- The waist area is larger than average/ideal.
- There is little or no indentation at the waist.
- A larger waist is characteristic of rectangular, rounded and diamond shaped body types and can occur in combination with above average/ideal weight, with a short midriff, midriff bulge and/or prominent abdomen.

Fitting Problem
- There is not enough fabric width to fit comfortably around the waist.
- The edges of the garment opening do not meet.
- If forced to meet and fasten, the tight waistband or waistline seam cuts into the body uncomfortably.
- In skirts, a tight horizontal fold forms all around the waist as fabric rides up, seeking a smaller area. Skirts can then appear too short.

- In pants, the horizontal fold may be smaller or fail to form at all, as fabric binds against the crotch.

Fabric & Pattern Alteration
- The garment needs more fabric to fit around the larger waist.
- Widen (let out) the side seams of bodice, skirt or pant at the waist and taper into original seam.
- Make waistband longer.

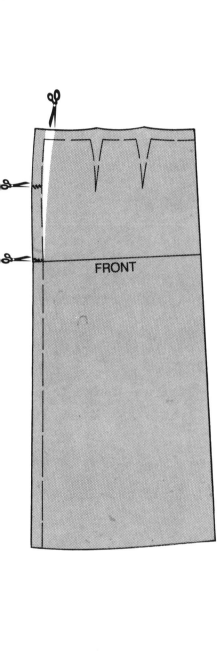

Fashions to Fit & Flatter

General Guidelines
- Camouflage or draw attention up and away from a large waist to create the illusion of a smaller waist.
- Clothes that require little or no alteration include waistless or loose-fitting garments between bust and hip.

Design Details & Specific Styling
- Wide V- and boat necklines; collars open at the neckline.
- Wide shoulder lines and shoulder pads.
- Fullness in the upper sleeve, including pleated, puffed, flared, butterfly and leg-o-mutton sleeves.
- Bloused tops or soft fullness above and below the waist.
- 1" waistbands.
- Waistless garments, such as an overblouse, tunic or tabard; shift, chemise and dropped waist dress or jumper.
- Longer sweater, vests and jackets.
- A-line, flare and circle skirts.
- Pleat-front or slight fullness in pants.

Accessories
- 1" to 2" belts with center front interest.
- Scarf at the neck or shoulders.
- Interesting jewelry near the face.

Avoid
- Exposing or emphasizing a larger waist with sleeves full at the elbow.
- Form-fitted midriffs or midriff yokes and blouses tucked in tight.
- High waistlines, wide waistbands.
- Short vests, sweaters and jackets.
- Box pleated, pegged and bouffant skirts.
- Harem, bloomer and hip-hugger pants.
- Heavy, bulky fabric around the waist.
- Horizontal stripes or bands.
- Wide belts.

Smaller Waist

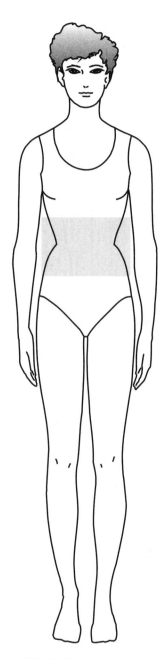

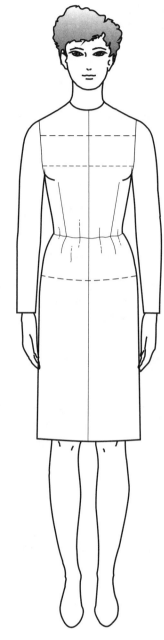

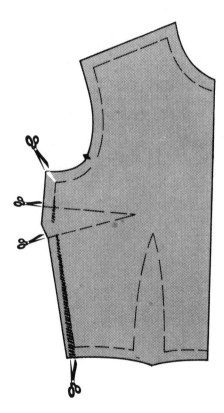

Figure Variation

- The waist area is smaller than average.
- There is an obvious indentation at the waist.
- A smaller waist is characteristic of ideal and hourglass shaped body types, and may occur in combination with a thin figure or prominent bust and large hips.
- The waist can actually be average/ideal, but appear small in proportion to large hips.

Fitting Problem

- There is too much fabric width to fit attractively around the waist.
- The edges of the garment opening overlap more than necessary.
- When fastened, the garment waist may stand loosely away from the body or drop down to rest on the larger hip area, with the garment curves positioned below the corresponding body curves including crotch in pants.

- Loose vertical ripples may be seen in the upper hip area.
- Hem positions may appear too large and long.

Fabric & Pattern Alteration

- The garment needs less fabric to fit around the smaller waist.
- Decrease (take in) garment width at side seams of bodice, skirt or pant at the waist and taper into original seam.
- Make waistband shorter.
- Make any corresponding bodice equally smaller in the waist.

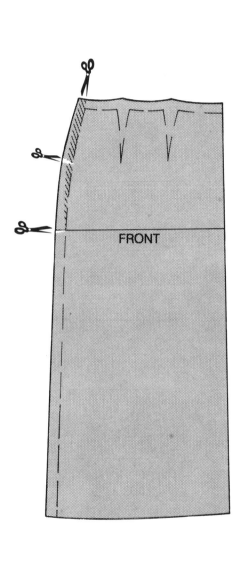

Fashions to Fit & Flatter

General Guidelines
- Camouflage or draw attention outward from a proportionally small waist to create the illusion of a larger waist—only if you need to balance a proportionally large bust and/or hips or buttocks, thus creating the illusion of smaller bust and hip areas.
- Clothes that require little or no alteration include waistless or loose-fitting garments between bust and hip.

Design Details & Specific Styling
- Wide shoulder lines; shoulder pads.
- Fullness in the upper sleeve and at the elbow.
- Fitted midriff and hip yokes.
- Wide waistbands.
- Short jackets and weskits.
- Tops bloused at the waist.
- Waistless garments, such as an overblouse, tunic, shift, chemise and dropped waist dress or jumper.
- Fullness in the lower edge of the skirt, including A-line, flare and circle skirts.
- Pleat-front pants; hip-huggers, harem, and drawstring pants.

Accessories
- To minimize - loose, narrow to medium width belts.
- To emphasize - wide and decorative belts, cummerbunds and cinch belts.

Avoid
- Emphasizing a small waist with
- Form-fitting midriffs, yokes, waistlines and hip yokes.
- Wide, tight belts.

Special Note: A small or narrow waist is generally a fashion asset. If you choose to emphasize a proportionally pleasing small waist, select from the styles and design details listed above. Skirts and pants selected to fit a small waist can be too tight in the hips.

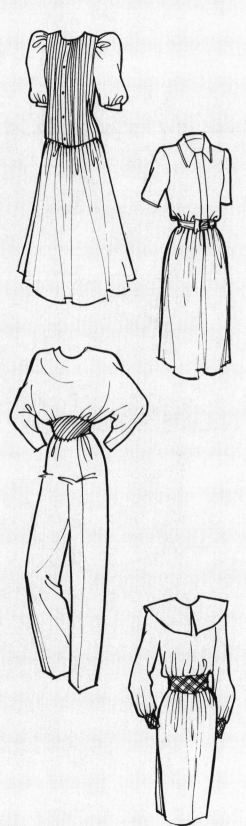

Sleeves

This section deals with selected figure variations occurring in the arms, and with fitting problems that result in garment sleeves. Figure variations that involve the entire arm are presented first, followed by variations arranged according to their vertical position on the arm. For example, figure variations in the upper arm are presented first, followed by a variation in the elbow.

Longer Arms

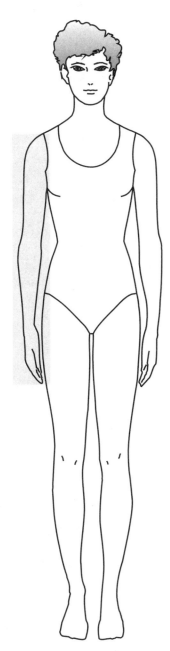

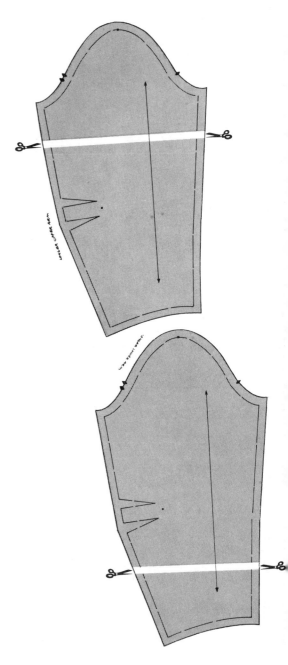

Figure Variation

• The arm bones are longer than average/ideal.
• Increased length can occur in the upper arm, lower arm, or be distributed between both.
• It is possible for the arms to be average in total length, but the upper arm can be proportionally longer than the lower arm, and vice versa.

Fitting Problem

• There is not enough fabric length to cover the arm attractively.
• The sleeve hem edge may not reach the desired level on the arm.
• If the upper arm is longer, the elbow dart(s) will be positioned above the elbow.
• If sleeve fullness or shaping is positioned too high, the sleeve can feel tight and uncomfortable.

Fabric & Pattern Alteration

• The garment needs more length to position the elbow dart(s) over the elbow and/or the hem at an attractive level.
• Lengthen (let down) the garment evenly at the hem, also the pattern can be lengthened evenly at approximately mid-upper and/or mid-lower arm, or both.
• If necessary on long sleeves, lower the elbow dart(s).

Fashions to Fit & Flatter

General Guidelines
- Camouflage, balance, or draw attention up or away from long arms to create the illusion of shorter arms.
- Clothes that require little or no alteration include three-quarter and shorter sleeves.

Design Details & Specific Styling
- Interesting necklines.
- Layered sleeves; loose-fitting and fuller sleeves, including puff, Juliet or peasant, cape, flounce and lantern sleeves; roll-up, push-up and three-quarter sleeves.
- Wide or contrasting color cuffs.
- Horizontal stripes in the sleeves.

Accessories
- Larger bracelets.
- Larger rings.

Avoid
- Exposing or emphasizing long arms in sleeveless tops; cap or tight-fitting sleeves; long sleeves that are too short or so long they hang over past the wrist.
- Vertical stripes in the sleeves.

Special Note: If any part of your lower torso (abdomen, buttocks, hips, thighs) is proportionally larger, review the appropriate sections. Some of the styles that flatter longer arms may not flatter those areas and therefore cancel some of the above advice.

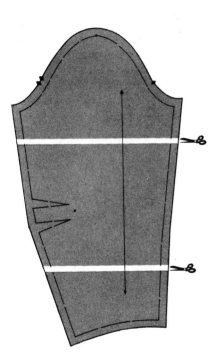

Shorter Arms

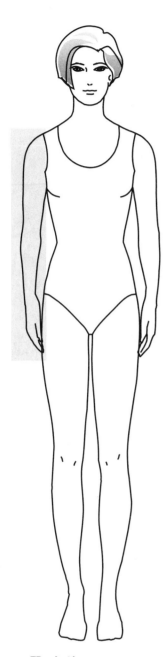

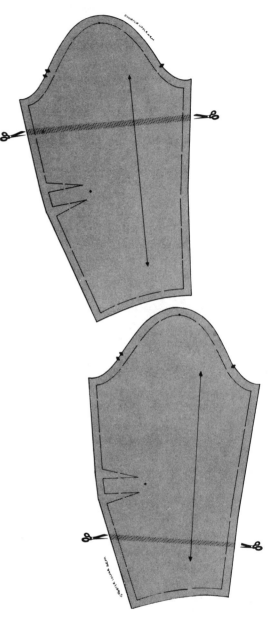

Figure Variation
- The arm bones are shorter than average/ideal.
- Decreased length can occur in the upper arm, lower arm, or be distributed between both.
- It is possible for the arms to be average in total length, but the upper arm can be proportionally shorter than the lower arm, and vice-versa.

Fitting Problem
- There is too much fabric length to cover the arm attractively.
- The sleeve hem edge may not reach the desired level on the arm.
- If the upper arm is shorter, the elbow dart(s) will be positioned below the elbow.
- If sleeve fullness or shaping is positioned too low, the sleeve will appear too loose.

Fabric & Pattern Alteration
- The garment needs less length to position the elbow dart(s) over the elbow and/or the hem at an attractive level.
- Shorten (take up) the garment evenly at the hem. Also, the pattern can be shortened evenly at approximately mid-upper and/or mid-lower arm, or both.
- If necessary on long sleeves, raise the elbow dart(s).

Fashions to Fit & Flatter

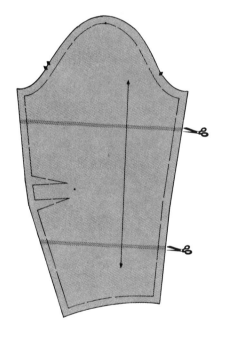

General Guidelines
- Camouflage, balance, or draw attention away from short arms to create the illusion of longer arms.
- Clothes that require little or no alteration include 7/8 and shorter sleeves.

Design Details & Specific Styling
- Sleeveless tops; cap, butterfly, three-quarter, kimono, raglan and dolman sleeves; narrower shirt-style and long fitted sleeves; long sleeves hemmed 1/4" to 1/2" beyond the wrist bone.
- Narrow cuffs, bands or binding.
- Vertical stripes in sleeves.

Accessories
- Narrow bracelets.
- Smaller rings.

Avoid
- Emphasizing or overwhelming shorter arms with heavy-layered sleeves; full sleeves including melon, lantern and flounced or low-ruffled sleeves.
- Wide or contrasting color cuffs.
- Heavy textured fabrics in sleeves.
- Horizontal stripes and border prints in sleeves.
- Wide bracelets.
- Large rings.

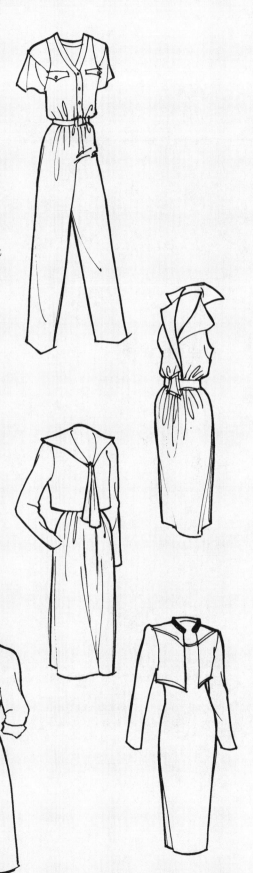

Larger Arms

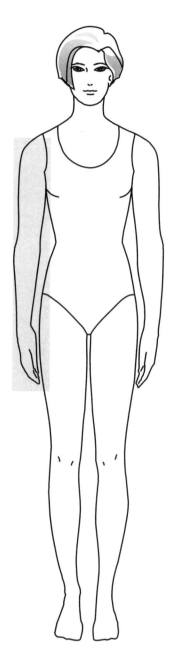

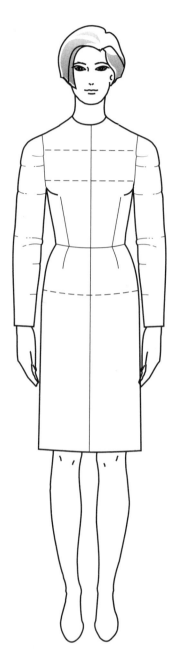

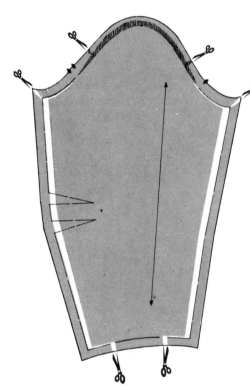

Figure Variation
- The arm bones are larger or carry more weight than average/ideal.
- Weight can be deposited on the upper arm, lower arm, at the wrist or be distributed evenly over the entire arm—as assumed in this discussion.
- Larger arms can be characteristic of an inverted triangular body type and occur in combination with a larger bust or above average/ideal weight.

Fitting Problem
- There is not enough fabric width to fit comfortably and attractively around the arm.
- Tight, horizontal ripples or wrinkles may form around the arm.
- The front and back armhole seam may pull toward the arm.
- The sleeve may appear too short.

Fabric & Pattern Alteration
- The garment sleeve needs more fabric width to fit the larger arm.
- Widen (let out) the garment sleeve at the sides, tapering into the original seam at the top of the sleeve cap. (The sleeve cap is lower to accommodate less shoulder angle.
- Also see *Larger Upper Arms.*

Fashions to Fit & Flatter

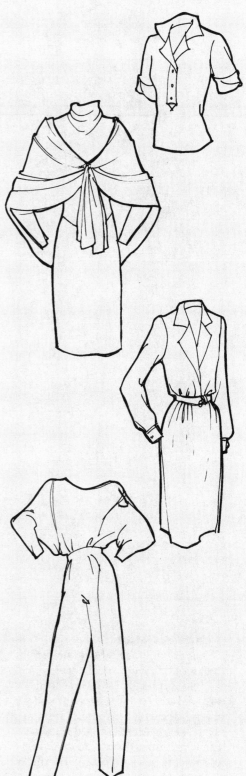

General Guidelines
- Camouflage, balance, or draw attention away from large or heavy arms to create the illusion of smaller arms.
- Clothes that require little or no alteration feature loose-fitting sleeves.

Design Details & Specific Styling
- Interesting necklines; medium to wide lapels.
- Broad shoulder lines and details; subtle shoulder pads.
- Medium to longer and loose-fitting sleeves, including camp, roll-up, three-quarter, kimono, raglan, dolman, shirt-style and bishop sleeves.
- Blouson tops and dresses; loose-fitting dresses.
- Light to medium weight fabrics that hold their shape.
- Narrow vertical lines and small patterns.

Accessories
- Shawls.

Avoid
- Exposing or emphasizing large or heavy arms with bulky shoulder pads.
- Sleeveless and strapless garments; cap and full-rounded or gathered sleeves including puff, melon and lantern styles.
- Wide cuffs.
- Tight-fitting or tightly tucked in tops.
- Clingy, thick or heavy fabrics in sleeves.
- Horizontal stripes or border prints in sleeves.
- Big, bulky upper arm bands or bracelets.

Smaller/Thin Arms

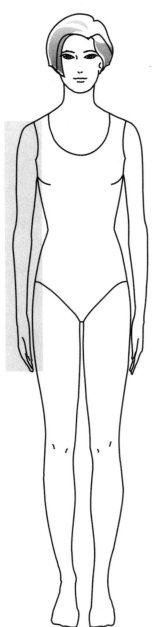

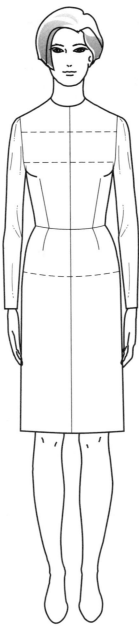

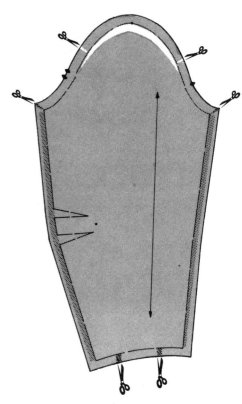

Figure Variation
- The arm bones are smaller or carry less weight than average/ideal.
- Weight can be deposited on the upper arm, lower arm, at the wrist or be distributed evenly over the entire arm—as assumed in this discussion.
- Small or thin arms can be characteristic of a triangular body type and occur in combination with a smaller bust or below average/ideal weight.

Fitting Problem
- There is too much fabric width to fit comfortably and attractively around the arm.
- Loose vertical ripples or wrinkles may form around the arm.
- The sleeve may appear slightly long.

Fabric & Pattern Alteration
- The garment sleeve needs less fabric width to fit the smaller arm.
- Narrow (take in) the garment sleeve at the sides, tapering into the original seam at the top of the sleeve cap. Increased height in sleeve cap accommodates more anular shoulder.

Fashions to Fit & Flatter

General Guidelines
- Camouflage, balance, or draw attention away from small or thin arms to create the illusion of larger arms.
- Clothes that require little or no alteration feature loose-fitting sleeves.

Design Details & Specific Styling
- Interesting necklines; portrait and cape collars.
- Epaulets and shoulder pads.
- Drop-shoulder sleeves; soft-fullness, flowing or draped sleeves, including leg-of-mutton, dolman or Bishop sleeves; three-quarter, roll-up or push-up sleeves.
- Pockets on the upper sleeve.
- Medium to wide cuffs.
- Lightweight layered looks.
- Light to medium weight, pliable and textured fabrics in sleeves.
- Horizontal stripes and border print sleeves.

Accessories
- Neck scarves and shawls.
- Narrow watch bands and bracelets.
- Small to medium rings.

Avoid
- Exposing or emphasizing thin arms with tight, form-fitting sleeves; full-rounded sleeves, including puff, butterfly, cape, and melon styles.
- Spaghetti strap or camisole tops.
- Thick, bulky fabrics in sleeves.
- Wide vertical stripes in sleeves.
- Large, heavy, bulky bracelets.
- Large rings.
- Large, bulky handbags with wide shoulder straps.

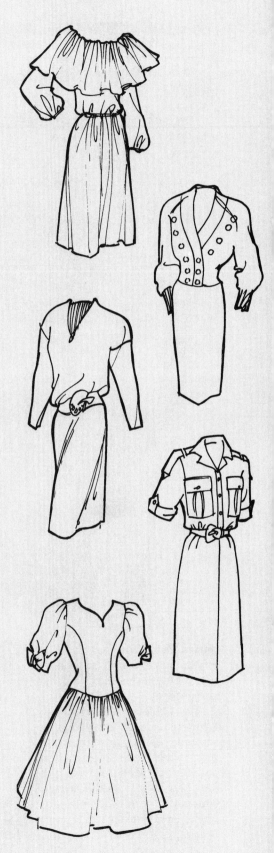

Larger Upper Arms

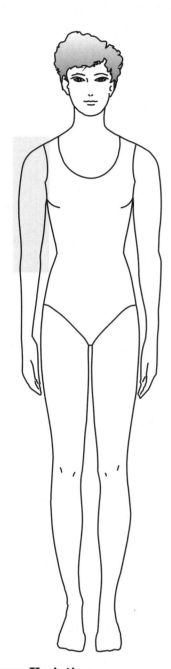

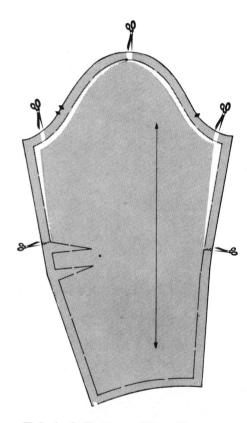

Figure Variation

- Only the upper arm bone or muscle is larger or carries more weight than average/ideal.
- Weight can be deposited on the front or back of the arm. Loss of muscle tone can cause the flesh to sag.
- Larger upper arms can be characteristic of an inverted triangular body type and occur in combination with a larger bust or above average/ideal weight.

Fitting Problem

- There is not enough fabric width to fit comfortably or attractively around the upper arm.
- Tight horizontal ripples or wrinkles form around the upper arm only.
- The front and back armhole seam may pull toward the arm.
- The sleeve may appear slightly short.

Fabric & Pattern Alteration

- The garment sleeve needs more fabric width to fit around the larger upper arm.
- Widen (let out) the garment sleeve sides at the capline and taper into the original seam at the elbow and at the top of the sleeve cap.
- Also see *Larger Arms*.

Fashions to Fit & Flatter

General Guidelines
- Camouflage, balance, and draw attention down or away from large or heavy upper arms to create the illusion of smaller upper arms.
- Clothes that require little or no alteration feature loose-fitting sleeves.

Design Details & Specific Styling
- Interesting necklines; medium to wide lapels.
- Broad shoulder looks and subtle shoulder pads.
- Medium to longer and loose-fitting sleeves, including camp, roll-up, three-quarter, kimono, raglan, dolman, shirt-style and Bishop sleeves.
- Light to medium weight fabrics that hold their shape.
- Narrow vertical lines and small patterns.

Accessories
- Shawls.
- Medium scale bracelets and rings.

Avoid
- Exposing or emphasizing large or heavy upper arms with bulky shoulder pads.
- Sleeveless and strapless garments; cap and full-rounded or gathered sleeves including puff, melon and lantern styles.
- Wide cuffs.
- Tight-fitting or tightly tucked in tops.
- Clingy, thick or heavy fabrics in sleeves.
- Horizontal stripes or border prints.
- Bulky upper arm bands or bracelets.

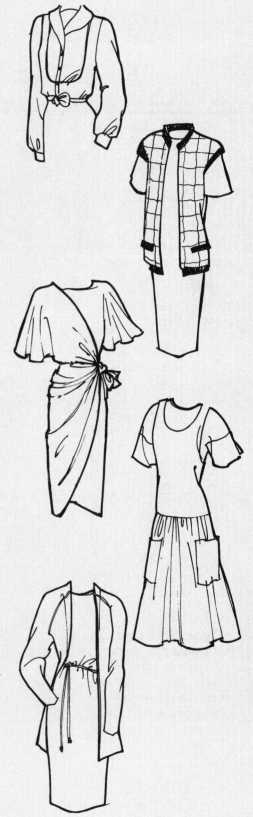

Inward Rotation of the Elbow

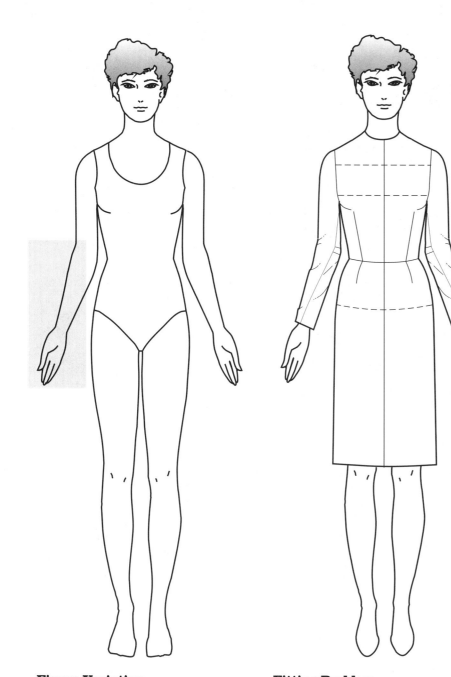

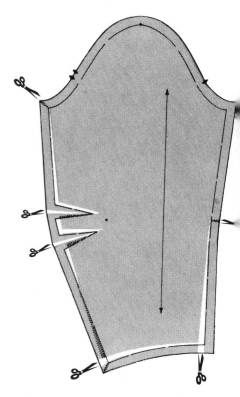

Figure Variation
- When the arms hang at the sides of the body in a relaxed position, the elbows bend inward and the hands hang away from the body, with palms turned forward.

Fitting Problem
- The garment sleeve will not lie on straight grain.
- Long sleeves twist around the lower arm and the underarm seam lines up with the thumb.
- The sleeve may pull tight between the elbow and wrist.

Fabric & Pattern Alteration
- The sleeve seam needs to be moved back.
- Let out the sleeve front seam and take in the sleeve back seam.
- Lengthen and widen the elbow area, including the dart(s).

Fashions to Fit & Flatter

General Guidelines
- Camouflage, balance, or draw attention up or away from inwardly rotated elbows to create the illusion of straighter arms.
- Clothes that require little or no alteration feature three-quarter and shorter sleeves, and flared or full-draped long sleeves without bands or cuffs.

Design Details & Specific Styling
- Interesting necklines and collars.
- Interesting shoulder lines; shoulder pads and epaulets.
- Loosely styled long sleeves.
- Roll sleeves up.

Accessories
- Interesting necklaces and pins.
- Interesting scarves.
- Narrow to medium, basic belts.

Avoid
- Exposing or emphasizing inwardly rotated elbows in strapless or sleeveless garments.
- Attention-getting belts.
- Attention-getting bracelets.

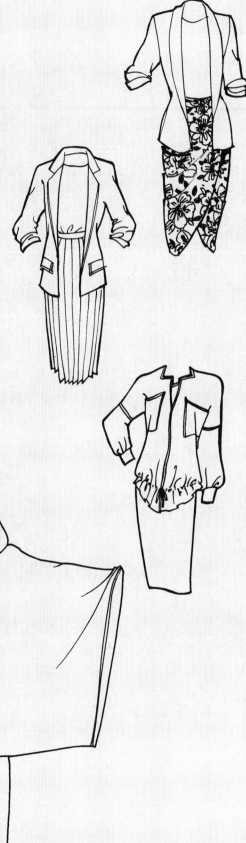

Skirts & Pants

Figure variations occurring in the lower torso and legs that result in fitting problems in skirts and pants are covered in this section. Figure variations are arranged according to their approximate vertical position on the body, starting from the waist and moving downward. For example, figure variations in the hip area are presented before variations in the thighs, knees, and so on.

Longer Lower Torso

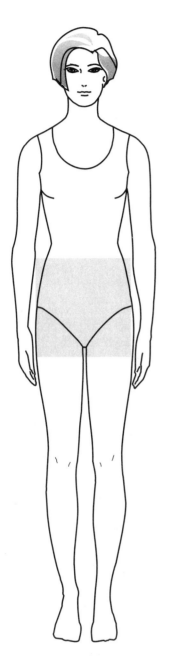

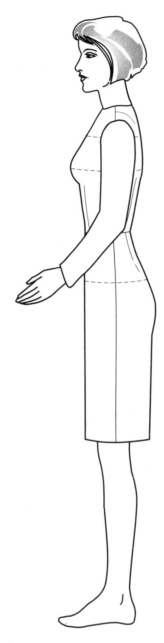

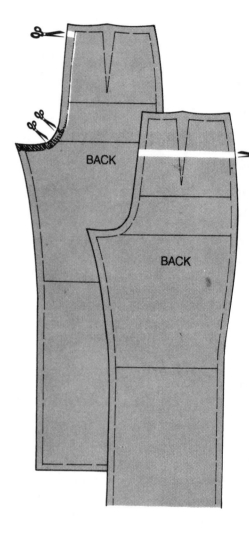

Figure Variation

- The pelvic bone structure in the lower torso, from waist to crotch, is longer than average/ideal.
- The hip curve and buttocks are positioned lower than average.
- The legs can be, or appear to be, shorter in proportion to the longer torso.

Fitting Problem

- The curve, shaping or fullness of the garment is positioned above the corresponding body curves—hip and buttocks.
- In skirts, there is slightly more width than required, just above the skirt hipline.
- In skirts, loose vertical ripples may form in back.

- In pants, diagonal wrinkles may form as fabric is pulled uncomfortably tight in the crotch, in front from crotch to hip bones, and in back from crotch to buttocks. (Do not confuse these wrinkles with those formed by high hip bones.)
- In pants, waistband may pull down, or hemline may pull up in back.

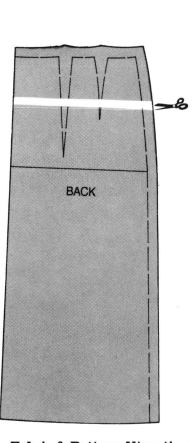

Fabric & Pattern Alteration
•The garment needs more fabric length to cover the lengthwise area between waist and crotch and to position garment shaping lower on skirt and pants, corresponding to the body curves.
•Lengthen (raise) the lower torso area, front and back.
•Lengthen the darts.
•Lower the crotch seam if necessary.

Fashions to Fit & Flatter

General Guidelines
•Camouflage, balance or draw attention away from a longer lower torso to create the illusion of a shorter waist to hip area.
•Clothes that require little or no alteration include loosely-styled skirts, dresses, jumpers, tunics or tabards, and bikini bathing suits.

Design Details & Specific Styling
•Fitted or straight skirts worn with longer jackets, sweaters and vests.
•A peplum.
•Dropped waistlines and hip yokes in skirts and pants, including hip-hugger pants.
•Horizontal lines, stripes or a pattern at the hips; trim applied at the hips.
•Wide belts and cummerbund.

Avoid
Exposing or emphasizing a longer lower torso with:
•midriff yokes, high waistlines,
•vertical lines and stripes in pants.

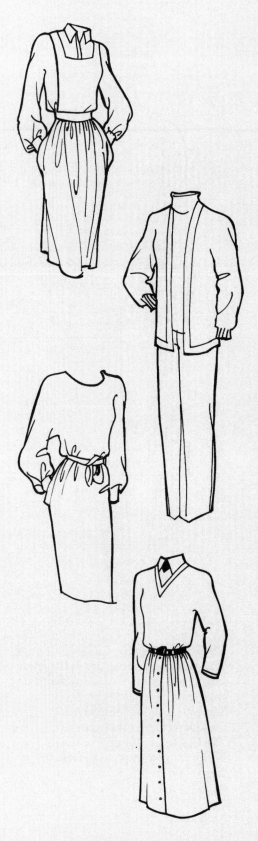

Short Lower Torso

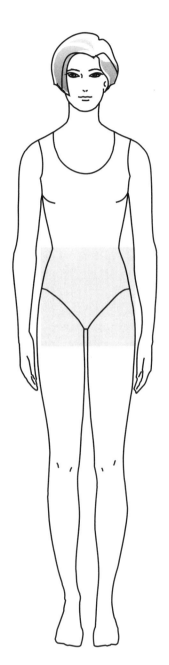

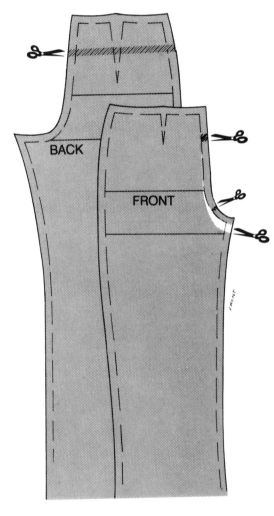

BACK

FRONT

Figure Variation

- The pelvic bone structure in the lower torso, from waist to crotch is shorter than average/ideal.
- The hip curve and buttocks are positioned higher than average.
- The legs can be, or appear to be, longer in proportion to the shorter torso.

Fitting Problem

- The curve, shaping or fullness of the garment is positioned below the corresponding body curves—hips and buttocks.
- There is not enough fabric width to fit smoothly around the hips and buttocks.
- Fabric is snug or strained across the back dart area.
- Side seams are pulled toward the back.

- Horizontal ripples or a fold may form across back darts as fabric rides above the buttocks. (Do not confuse with a fold formed by a sway back.)
- In pants, the crotch seam hangs too low, away from the body.
- Upper pant leg may appear too large in back.
- Pant legs may be too long.

Fashions to Fit & Flatter

General Guidelines
- Camouflage, balance or draw attention up and away from a shorter lower torso to create the illusion of a longer waist to hip area.
- Clothes that require little or no alteration include loosely-styled skirts, dresses, jumpers, tunics or tabards, and bikini bathing suits.

Design Details & Specific Styling
- Raised waistlines in skirts and pants.
- Irregular vertical lines in the hip area.
- Fitted or straight skirts with longer jackets, sweaters or vests.
- Raised waistlines, including shift, sheath, princess and empire waist dresses.
- Skirts pleated from the waist; gently flared and gored skirts; long skirts.

Accessories
- Narrow belts.

Avoid
- Exposing or emphasizing a shorter lower torso with hip yokes and hip-hugger pants.
- Horizontal lines and stripes in pants.

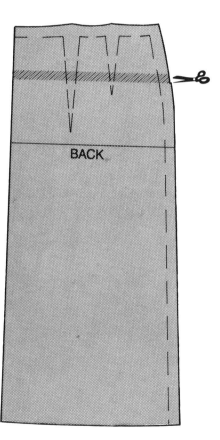

BACK

Fabric & Pattern Alteration
- The garment needs less fabric length to cover the lengthwise area between waist and crotch and to position garment shaping higher on skirt and pants, corresponding to the body curves.
- Shorten (lower) the lower torso area.
- Shorten the darts.
- Raise the crotch seam if necessary.

Larger Abdomen

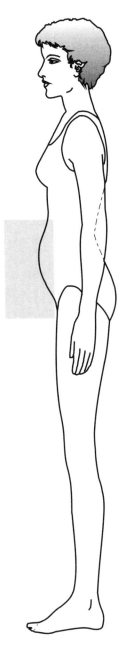
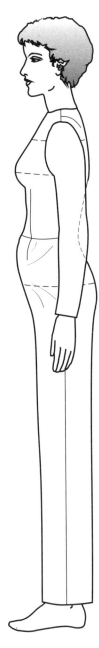
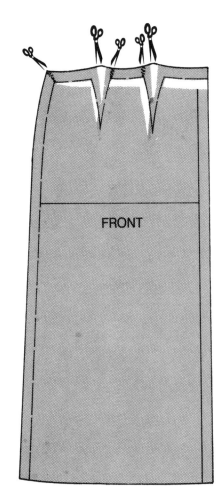

FRONT

Figure Variation

- The abdomen protrudes more than average/ideal.
- The abdominal curve rounds out just below the waist.
- Distance increases over the abdomen, between the waist and crotch at body center.
- A large abdomen is characteristic of triangular, diamond or rectangular body types and can occur in combination with above average/ideal weight, slumped posture, a short rib cage, midriff bulge or a large waist.

Fitting Problem

- There is not enough fabric length and width or curved shaping to fit attractively over the abdomen.
- The edges of a garment opening do not meet.
- If forced to meet and fasten, or if one piece, fabric pulls tight across the abdomen.
- In skirt front, a tight horizontal fold can form above the abdomen as fabric rides up.
- Side seams bow forward between the hip and waist.

- Tight diagonal ripples may form, angled toward the stomach curve.
- Fitted skirts and pants cut under the abdomen.
- Skirt hemline may be pulled up in front, causing hemline to poke out at the center.
- In pants, the crotch seam is pulled upward.
- In pants, vertical wrinkles often form between the crotch and abdomen as fabric is pulled uncomfortably tight.

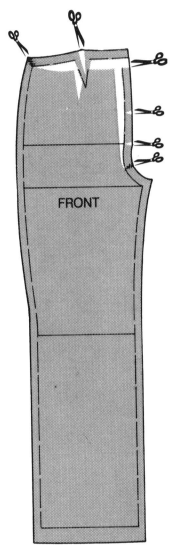

Fabric & Pattern Alteration
- The garment needs more fabric length and width, and more curved shaping to fit the larger abdomen attractively.
- Lengthen (raise) the garment front at the waist, tapering into original waistline at side seams.
- Widen (let out) the garment at side seams and/or center front.
- Lengthen and widen front darts.

Fashions to Fit & Flatter

General Guidelines
- Camouflage and draw attention up or away from the abdomen to create the illusion of a flatter tummy. Fill out the area above the tummy.
- Clothes that require little or no alteration include loose-fitting and waistless styles.

Design Details & Specific Styling
- Boatneck, bowed and cowl collars; a jabot.
- Bloused tops.
- Loose-fitting or waistless overblouses, tunics, dresses and jumpers; caftans.
- Longer, loose-fitting vests, sweaters and jackets; shorter vests and jackets when paired with flared or straight-hanging dirndl skirts.
- Flared and straight-hanging dirndl skirts; skirts with flat-lying, stitched-down knife pleats; skirts with gathers on either side of the stomach; longer skirts.
- Flat-lying pleat-front pants and palazzo pants.
- Layered looks.

Accessories
- Neckline and shoulder details; shoulder pads.
- Interesting earrings, pins and necklaces.
- Scarves at the neckline.
- Loose or low-slung belts.

Avoid
- Emphasizing a large tummy with Bishop sleeves and other sleeves with fullness at the wrist.
- Exposing a large tummy with form-fitted clothes of any type, including fitted midriffs, midriff yokes and sheath dresses.
- Short, fitted vests, sweaters and jackets, including bolero, aviator and battle jackets.
- Bulky knife-pleated or box-pleated skirts; button-front skirts; short skirts.
- Hip-hugger, harem and tapered pants; fitted jumpsuits.
- Bulky, shiny or clingy fabrics in skirts and pants.
- Tight or wide belts.

Flat Abdomen

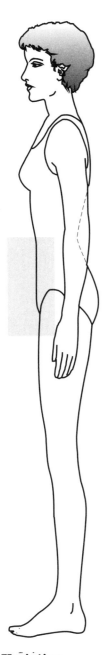

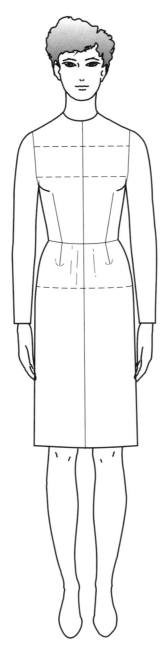

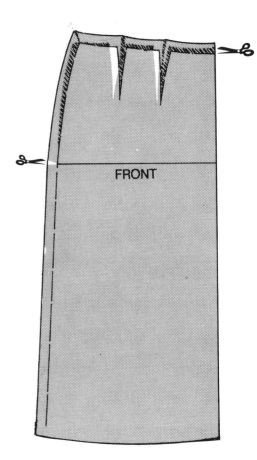

FRONT

Figure Variation
- The abdomen is flatter than average.
- There is no abdominal curve below the waist.
- Distance decreases over the abdomen, between waist and crotch at body center.
- A flat abdomen can be characteristic of an inverted triangular body type and can occur in combination with below average/ideal weight, a long rib cage, small waist or prominent hip bones.

Fitting Problem
- There is too much fabric length and width and curved shaping to fit attractively over the abdomen.
- Garment shaping or fullness hangs loose in front.
- Vertical ripples may form below the darts.
- Skirt hemline may sag at center front.
- In pants, the crotch seam may drop slightly.

Fabric & Pattern Alteration
- The garment needs less fabric length and width, and less curved shaping to fit the flat abdomen attractively.
- Shorten (lower) the garment front at the waist, tapering into original waistline at side seams.
- Narrow (take in) garment width at side seams and/or center front.
- Make front darts shorter and narrower. Eliminate center most front darts if the abdomen is completely flat.

Fashions to Fit & Flatter

General Guidelines
- Camouflage or fill out the abdominal area to create the illusion of a slight stomach curve.
- Clothes that require little or no alteration include loose-fitting or waistless styles.

Design Details & Specific Styling
- Overblouses, tunics, waistless jumpers and dresses.
- Longer, loose-fitting vests, sweaters and jackets.
- Gathered, softly pleated, unpressed pleated and flared skirts.
- Gathered or pleat-front pants, drawstring or palazzo pants.
- Knits and softly textured fabrics.

Accessories
- Softly tied sash around the waist.

Avoid
- Form-fitting skirts and pants if the variation occurs in combination with prominent hip bones.

Special Note: In most cases, this figure variation is an asset. Enjoy!

Sway Back

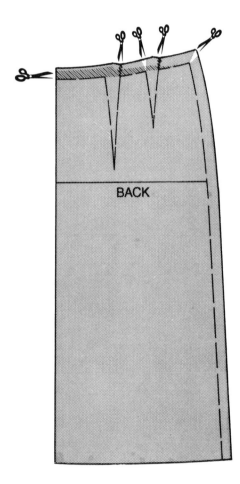

Figure Variation

- The top of the pelvis tilts forward, lifting the buttocks up and outward.
- In back, the buttocks protrude more than average/ideal.
- In front, the groin area indents more than average.
- Distance decreases between the waist and buttocks ("small" of the back).
- Distance increases between the buttocks and crotch at body center.
- A sway back can be lessened or eliminated by improved posture.

Fitting Problem

- In skirt back, there is too much fabric length between the buttocks and waist. In skirt back, a tapered horizontal fold may form just below the waist.
- Skirt hemline is pulled up in back, causing hemline to poke out at center back.
- In pants, a horizontal fold seldom forms. Instead, fabric binds against the crotch and is pulled tight under the buttocks.
- In pants, wrinkles may form which angle toward the inseam.
- In pants, the waistband may be pulled down in back.

Fabric & Pattern Alteration

- In skirts, the garment needs less fabric length between the back waist and buttocks.
- In skirt back, shorten (lower) the area just below the waist, tapering into original waistline at side seams.
- In pants, the garment needs more fabric through the crotch.

Fashions to Fit & Flatter

General Guidelines
- Camouflage, fill in, or draw attention up and away from a sway back to create the illusion of improved posture.
- Clothes that require little or no alteration feature a loose, full fit between the mid-back and buttocks.

Design Details & Specific Styling
- A low back-draped (below the waist) cowl neckline.
- Overblouses and tunics; bloused back bodices.
- Longer, loose fitting sweaters and vests.
- Longer, straight-hanging jackets, such as a box or Chanel jacket, car coat or poncho.
- Shift and A-line dresses; shirtwaist dresses bloused at the waist.
- Flared, dirndl, unpressed pleat or tiered skirts; a handkerchief hem.
- Layered looks.

Accessories
- A scarf or shawl at the neck.

Avoid
- Exposing or emphasizing swayed back posture with fitted midriffs and midriff yokes.
- Short or fitted vests, sweaters and jackets.
- Sheath and princess style dresses.
- Hip yokes, back pockets.
- Wide or cinch belts, and clingy fabric.

- In pants back, more fabric length may also be needed just below the waist.
- In pants, widen the back crotch extension, tapering into original inseam.
- In pants, if needed, lengthen back area between waist and buttocks, adjusting center back and side seams as required.
- Shorten skirt back darts and lengthen pants back darts as required.

Sway Front

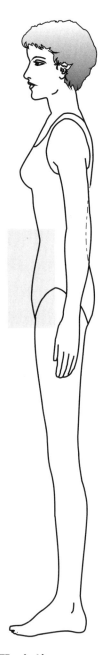

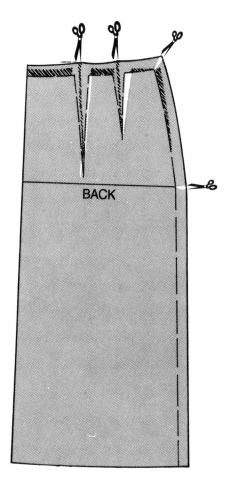

BACK

Figure Variation
- The top of the pelvis tilts backward,
- The buttocks protrude less than average/ideal.
- The waist appears to indent in front more than average.
- A sway front can occur in combination with a flat buttocks.
- A sway front can be lessened or eliminated by improved posture.

Fitting Problem
- In skirt back, there is too much fabric shaping and length below back darts.
- In skirt back, diagonal ripples form as fabric droops across buttocks.
- Skirt hemline droops against the back of the legs.
- Skirt side seams slant forward.
- Skirt hemline may round out in front.
- In pants, fabric sags under the buttocks.
- Pant side seams bow.

- In pants, droopy, diagonal wrinkles form across back crease lines.
- In pants, hemline droops in back and may rise in front.

Fabric & Pattern Alteration
- The garment needs less fabric length and curved shaping to fit the buttocks attractively.
- Shorten (lower) the area just below the waist, tapering into original waistline at side seams.

Fashions to Fit & Flatter

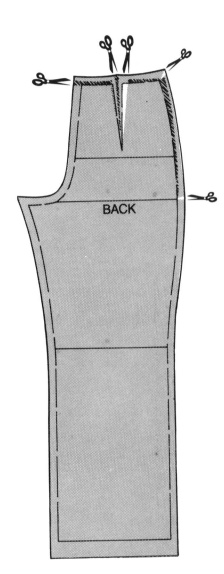

BACK

- Make back darts shorter and narrower for less curved shaping.
- Adjust side seams as required.
- In pants, deepen the back crotch curve if needed.
- When variation is extreme, increase fabric length in front.

General Guidelines
- Camouflage or draw attention up and away from a sway front to create the illusion of improved posture. Clothes that require little or no alteration feature a loose, full fit between the mid-back and hem.

Design Details & Specific Styling
- Front collar detail; notched collar open at front.
- Pleat-front blouses, overblouses and tunics; bloused front bodices.
- Longer, loose fitting sweaters and vests.
- Longer, unconstructed jackets; short jacket bloused in back only; car coat or poncho.
- Shift, A-line and shirtwaist dresses.
- Flared, gathered dirndl, unpressed pleat or tiered skirts; back-fullness in the skirt, as with a peplum or bustle effect.
- Layered looks.

Accessories
- A scarf or shawl.

Avoid
- Exposing or emphasizing swayed front posture with a fitted bodice or midriff yoke.
- Short or fitted vests, sweaters; fitted jackets.
- Sheath dresses.
- Hip yokes, front pockets on skirts and pants.
- Clingy fabric.
- Wide or cinch belts.

High Hip Curve (Square)

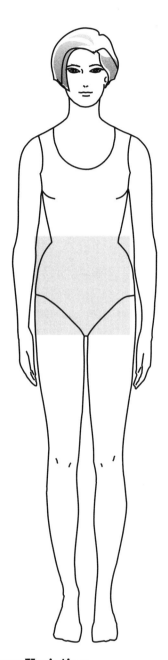

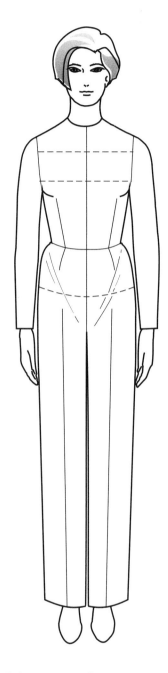

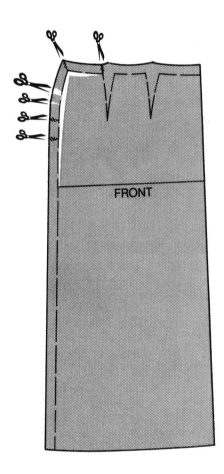

FRONT

Figure Variation
- The pelvic or hip curve is higher than average/ideal, about 3" below the waist.
- The upper hip curves abruptly outward just below the waist, then drops almost straight down.
- Excess weight is usually deposited on the hip bone in back and on the abdomen.

- A high hip curve is characteristic of an inverted-triangle body type, and often occurs in combination with a short rib cage, wide waist, flat buttocks and flat thighs at the sides.
- Legs can appear longer because of flat thighs at the sides.

Fitting Problem
- There is not enough fabric to fit around the upper hip curve.
- Fabric is tight around the upper hip curve.

- In a skirt, horizontal wrinkles or folds form all around, as fabric rides up. (Do not confuse this fold with a sway back, large waist or wide hips.)
- In pants, fabric often forms diagonal wrinkles as fabric is pulled tight between the crotch and upper hip. (Do not confuse these wrinkles with those formed by a long lower torso.)
- In pants, the hemline may pull up at the sides.

Fashions to Fit & Flatter

General Guidelines
- Camouflage and draw attention up and away from a high hip curve to make it less noticeable. Fill in the area below.
- Clothes that require little or no alteration include clothes with a loose fit or flare, at or below the waist.

Design Details & Specific Styling
- Interesting design lines and details in the neck and shoulder area.
- Waistless tops, overblouses and tunics.
- Longer vests, sweaters or jackets, particularly over fitted or straight skirts.
- Shift, chemise and other waistless jumpers or dresses.
- Elasticized waistlines; waistline elasticized in back only; soft gathers in place of darts at the waist.
- A-line, flared and straight-hanging dirndl skirts; pull-on skirts.
- Pull-on pants.

Accessories
- Narrow belts.
- Attention-getting earrings, pins and necklaces.
- A scarf, high on the figure.

Avoid
- Exposing or emphasizing a high hip curve with sheath and other form-fitting dresses.
- Short or fitted jackets, vests and sweaters.
- Dart-fitted straight skirts.
- Thick, bulky fabrics in skirts and pants.
- Large bracelets.
- Wide belts.

Fabric & Pattern Alteration
- The garment needs more fabric length and width to fit the curve of the upper hip area.
- Widen (let out) the garment in the upper hip area at side seams, tapering into original seamline at waist and low-hip level.
- Lengthen (raise) the garment side seams at the waist to fit out and over the high hip curve. Taper into original waistline.

Low Hip Curve (Sloped)

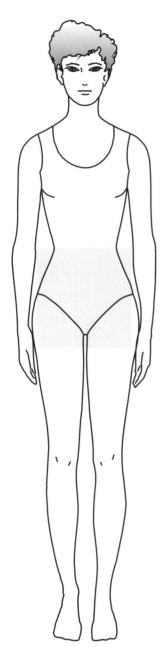

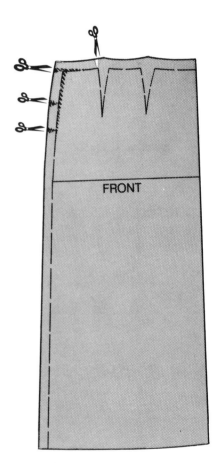

FRONT

Figure Variation

- The pelvic or hip curve is lower than average/ideal, about 9" to 10" below the waist.
- Hips gently slope or taper from the waist to the hip joint.
- Excess weight is usually deposited on the hip joint/upper thigh.
- A low hip curve is characteristic of a triangular body type and often occurs in combination with a longer rib cage, small waist, larger buttocks and wide thighs at the sides.

- Legs can appear proportionally shorter.

Fitting Problem

- There is too much fabric width on the sloped upper hip area.
- Loose vertical ripples may form in the upper hip area, near side seams.

Fabric & Pattern Alteration

- The garment may need less fabric width and length in the upper hip area.
- Decrease (take in) garment width in the mid-hip at side seams, tapering into original seamline at waist and low-hip level.
- If necessary, shorten (lower) side seams at the waist. Taper into original waistline.

Fashions to Fit & Flatter

General Guidelines
- Camouflage, balance, and draw attention up and away from a low hip curve to make it unnoticeable and to create the illusion of a smooth hip curve.
- Clothes that require little or no alteration include loose-fitting clothing, at or below the high hipline.

Design Details & Specific Styling
- Elasticized waistlines; soft gathers in place of darts at the waist.
- Longer vests, sweaters or jackets, particularly over fitted or straight skirts.
- Shift, chemise and other waistless jumpers and dresses.
- A-line, flared, gored and straight-hanging dirndl skirts.
- Layered looks.

Accessories
- Attention-getting earrings, pins and necklaces.
- Interesting design lines and details in the neck and shoulder area.
- A scarf, high on the figure.
- Mid to high heels and boots.

Avoid
- Form-fitting skirts and pants.

Special Note: If the low hip curve is very noticeable, see fashion advice for wider hips and thighs at sides.

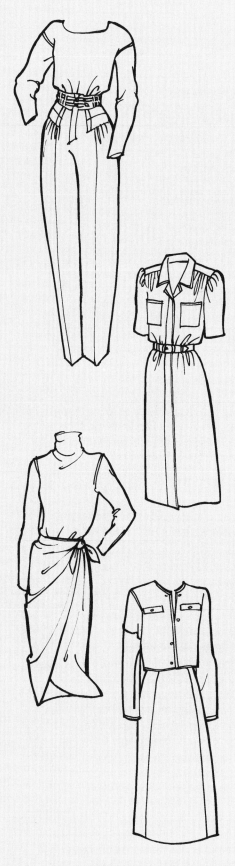

Wide Hips

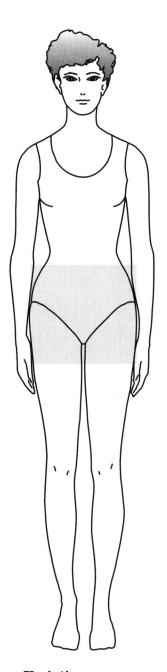

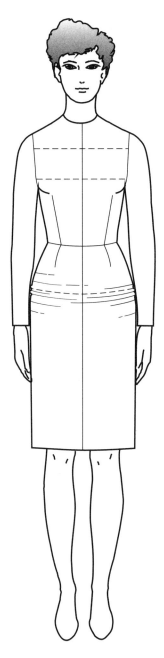

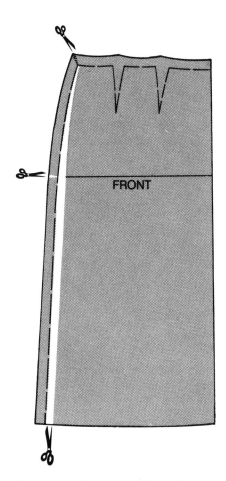

Figure Variation
- The pelvic or hip structure is larger and wider than average/ideal.
- Wide hips are characteristic of rectangular, triangular, rounded and hourglass body types and can appear in combination with a low hip curve, large thighs, or above average/ideal weight.
- Hips can actually be average/ideal, but appear wide in proportion to a small waist.

Fitting Problem
- There is not enough fabric width to fit around the hips.
- Fabric is tight around the widest part of the hips.
- In skirts, tight, horizontal ripples or folds can form around the hips and ride up around the waist.
- In pants, horizontal ripples can form around the hips at side, but fabric is held in place at center front and center back by the crotch.
- Skirts and pants selected to fit wide hips are often too large in the waist.

Fabric & Pattern Alteration
- The garment needs more fabric width to fit around larger, wider hips.
- Widen (let out) the garment side seams from hem to full hip level and taper into original seam at waist.
- In pants, additional width at hips may also be tapered into original leg if preferred.

Fashions to Fit & Flatter

General Guidelines
• Camouflage, balance or draw attention up and away from wider hips to create the illusion of narrower hips.
• Clothes that require little or no alteration feature a soft, loose or trim fit below the waist.

Design Details & Specific Styling
• Broad shoulder lines, shoulder pads, epaulets.
• Breast pockets; vertical or diagonal slot pockets at the hips.
• Overblouses and tunics; bloused tops and dress bodices.
• Longer, loose-fitting sweaters, vests.
• Longer, unconstructed jackets.
• Shift, chemise, flared, caftan and shirtwaist dresses.
• Flared or bias-cut A-line skirts; straight-hanging dirndl skirts; stitched-down, flat-lying pleated skirts.
• Longer hemlines.
• Straight-hanging or flared coats and capes.
• Layered looks.

Accessories
• Hats.
• Interesting earrings, pins or necklace.
• A bow or scarf at the neck or shoulders.
• Mid to high heels and boots.

Avoid
• Exposing and emphasizing wider hips in form-fitting clothes.
• Narrow shoulder lines.
• Horizontal slot and flap pockets at the hips.
• Side zippers and horizontal zippers at hips.
• Short jackets worn with straight skirts.
• Bulky bouffant, unpressed or open pleat skirts; pegged skirts; short hemlines.
• Bell-bottom, tapered and cuffed pants.

• Thick, bulky or clingy fabric in skirts and pants.
• Horizontal lines or stripes in hip area.
• Tight, wide belts.
• Large, bulky handbags.
• Heavy or chunky shoes.

Narrow Hips

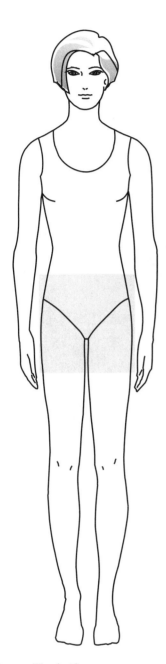

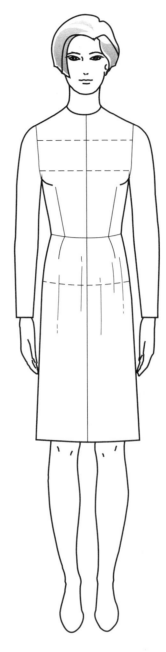

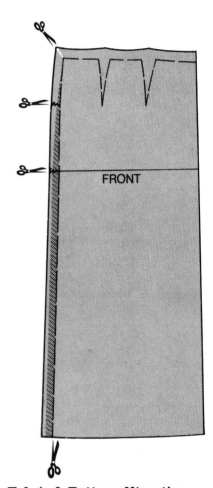

FRONT

Figure Variation

- The pelvic or hip structure is smaller and narrower than average/ideal.
- Narrow hips are characteristic of inverted triangle and diamond-shaped body types and can appear in combination with a high hip curve or below average/ideal weight.
- Hips may actually be average, but appear narrow in proportion to a large waist and/or midriff.

Fitting Problem

- There is too much fabric width around the hips.
- Fabric is loose around the widest part of the hips.
- Loose vertical ripples can form all around the hips.
- Pants may hang too loose and low in the crotch.
- Skirts and pants selected to fit narrow hips can be too small in the waist.

Fabric & Pattern Alteration

- The garment needs less fabric width to fit around smaller, narrower hips.
- Decrease (take in) garment width at side seams from hem to full hip level and taper into original seam at the waist.
- In pants, decreased width at hips can also be tapered into original leg if preferred.

Fashions to Fit & Flatter

General Guidelines
- Camouflage, balance or fill out narrow hips to create the illusion of proportionally wider hips.
- Clothes that require little or no alteration feature a loose or full fit below the waist.

Design Details & Specific Styling
- Tight-fitted midriff and waist areas.
- Peplums.
- A shirred hip yoke.
- Side zippers.
- Horizontal slot and patch pockets in hip area.
- Short and mid-length hemlines.
- Sleeveless tops, crop-tops, belted overblouses and tunics.
- Short to mid-hip length vests, sweaters and jackets.
- Box, bolero, aviator, blouson and double-breasted jackets.
- Drop-waist and princess and shirtwaist dresses.
- Pegged, flared and gored skirts; dirndl, bouffant and pleated skirts; draped, tiered or ruffled skirts.
- Pleat-front, baggy, bell-bottom, tapered and cuffed pants; loose-fitting jumpsuits.
- Double-breasted or belted coats and capes.
- Layered looks.
- Soft or textured, medium-weight fabrics.
- Horizontal lines or stripes in hip area.

Accessories
- Medium to wide belts, cinch belts, sashes and fanny wraps; tight, wide belts.
- Low, ankle boots.

Avoid
- Exposing or emphasizing narrower hips with vertical slot pockets.
- Oversized tops.
- Form-fitted skirts and pants.
- Clingy or flimsy fabrics.
- Horizontal stripes in tops and vertical lines or stripes in straight skirts or pants.

Larger Buttocks

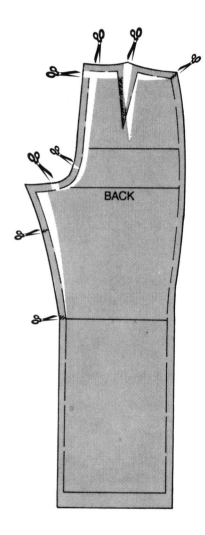

BACK

Figure Variation

- The buttocks are larger and curve outward more than average/ideal.
- Distance increases over the buttocks, between the waist and crotch at body center.
- Hip circumference increases.
- Larger buttocks are characteristic of triangle and rounded body types and often occur in combination with above average/ideal weight.

Fitting Problem

- There is not enough fabric length and width, and curved shaping to fit attractively.
- Strained fabric pulls tight across the buttocks.
- Side seams bow backward at low hip level.
- Tight diagonal ripples can form, angled toward the buttocks curve.
- Strained fabric cups under the abdomen and/or buttocks.

- Skirt hemline can be pulled up in back, causing hemline to poke out at the center.
- In pants, the waistband may be pulled down in back.
- In back pant leg, diagonal wrinkles can form, angled towards the crotch.

Fabric & Pattern Alteration

- The garment needs more fabric length and width, and more curved shaping to fit larger buttocks attractively.

Fashions to Fit & Flatter

General Guidelines
- Camouflage, balance or draw attention up and away from larger buttocks or behind, to create the illusion of a smaller behind.
- Clothes that require little or no alteration feature a loose fit below the mid-back and/or soft fullness below the waist.

Design Details & Specific Styling
- Interesting collars.
- Broad shoulder lines, shoulder pads, epaulets.
- Boatneck, backless and halter tops, bloused tops and overblouses.
- Longer, loose-fitting vests, sweaters and jackets.
- Loose-fitting or waistless tunics, jumpers and dresses; caftans.
- Flared and softly gathered, straight-hanging dirndl skirts; longer skirts.
- Straight-leg and palazzo pants; slightly loose Bermuda shorts.
- Full-cut and flared coats.
- Layered looks.
- Dull finish, flatter fabrics.

Accessories
- Scarves at the neck and chest.
- Narrow belts.
- Simple, mid-height high heels or boots.

Avoid
- Exposing or emphasizing a larger behind with form-fitting clothes.
- Extremely fussy, frilly, ruffled necklines and collars.
- Bishop sleeves.
- Form-fitted midriffs and midriff yokes.
- Tight or wide waistbands.
- A short peplum; back vents
- Decorative back pockets.
- Short, fitted vests, sweaters and jackets; bolero, aviator and battle jackets.
- Sheath dresses.
- Form-fitted skirts, bouffant, pegged, button-back and box- or knife-pleated skirts.
- Hip-hugger, harem, tapered pants, fitted jumpsuits and short shorts.
- Belted coats.
- Shiny, clingy or bulky fabrics in skirts and pants.
- Wide or tight belts.
- Chunky shoes.

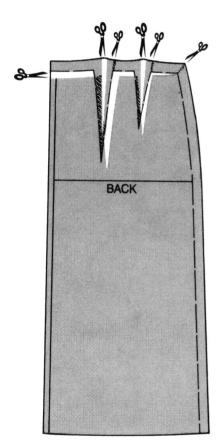

- Lengthen (raise) the garment at the waist in back, tapering into original waistline at side seams.
- Widen (let out) the garment at side seams and/or center back.
- Lengthen and widen back darts.
- In pants, widen the back crotch extension.

Smaller/Flat Buttocks

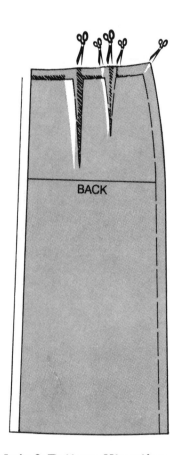

Figure Variation

- The buttocks are smaller and flatter than average/ideal.
- Distance decreases over the buttocks, between the waist and crotch at body center.
- Hip circumference decreases.
- Small or flat buttocks are characteristic of inverted triangle and diamond-shaped body types and can occur in combination with below average/ideal weight.

Fitting Problem

- There is too much fabric length and width, and curved shaping to fit attractively .
- Garment shaping or fullness hangs loose in back, forming vertical ripples below back darts.
- Skirt hemline may sag at center back.
- In back pant leg, diagonal ripples can form as fabric droops.

Fabric & Pattern Alteration

- The garment needs less fabric length and width, and less curved shaping to fit a small or flat buttocks attractively.
- Shorten (lower) the garment at the waist in back, tapering into original waistline at side seams.
- Decrease (take in) garment width at side seams and/or center back.
- Make back darts shorter and narrower.
- In pants, decrease the back crotch extension, if necessary.

Fashions to Fit & Flatter

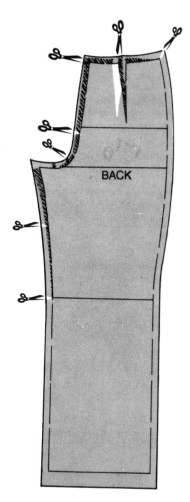

General Guidelines
- Camouflage, fill out or draw attention up and away from smaller or flat buttocks to create the illusion of more curvaceous buttocks.
- Clothes that require little or no alteration include loose-fitting or waistless clothes.

Design Details & Specific Styling
- V-back neckline.
- Peplums.
- Patch and decorative back pockets.
- Belted overblouses and tunics.
- Longer, loose-fitting or belted vests and sweaters.
- Longer, fitted, belted and blouson jackets; car coat or poncho.
- Shift, chemise, A-line, shirtwaist and drop-waist dresses.
- Flared, gored, and dirndl skirts; box-pleat and unpressed pleated skirts; bouffant or tiered skirts; split skirts.
- Harem, baggy, drawstring or palazzo pants.
- Layered looks.

Accessories
- Interesting earrings, pins or necklace.
- A scarf or shawl.
- Crushed socks.
- Ankle boots.

Avoid
- Exposing or emphasizing small or flat buttocks with tops bloused in back.
- Sheath dresses.
- Aviator or short blouson jackets.
- Dart-fitted straight skirts.
- Form-fitted pants.
- Clingy fabric.

Larger Thighs at the Outside

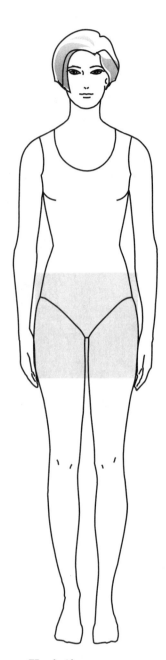

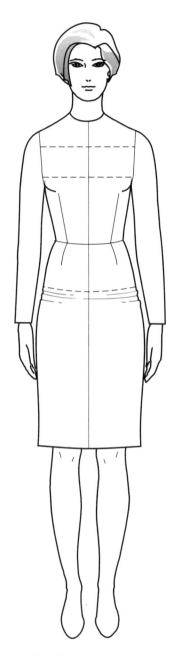

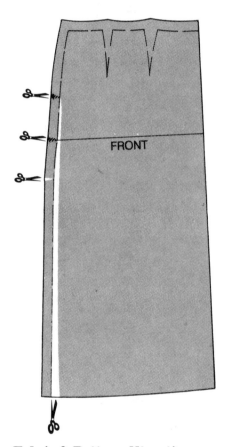

FRONT

Figure Variation

- Thighs are larger at the outside than average/ideal.
- Excess weight is deposited on upper thighs at the outside, just below the hipline.
- Larger thighs at the outside are characteristic of a triangle-shaped figure type, possibly in combination with a low hip curve.

Fitting Problem

- There is not enough fabric width to go around the upper thighs.
- Fabric is tight around the upper thighs.
- Tight horizontal ripples or a fold may form around the upper thighs, just below the hipline.
- In pants, horizontal ripples may form from the crotch, radiating toward the outside thigh.
- In pants, creases are pulled outward at the upper thigh.
- Fabric cups under thighs and buttocks.

Fabric & Pattern Alteration

- The garment needs more fabric width to fit around larger thighs.
- Widen (let out) the garment side seams from hem to full thigh level and taper into the original seam at mid-hip.
- In pants, additional width at thighs may also be tapered into original leg if preferred.

Fashions to Fit & Flatter

General Guidelines
- Camouflage, balance or draw attention up and away from larger thighs to create the illusion of narrower thighs.
- Clothes that require little or no alteration feature a soft, loose fit below the mid-hip.

Design Details & Specific Styling
- V- and bowed necklines; interesting collars.
- Broad shoulder lines and shoulder pads; epaulets.
- Dolman sleeves.
- Breast pockets and vertical slot pockets.
- Overblouses and tunics; bloused tops and dress bodices.
- Longer, loose-fitting sweaters and vests.
- Longer, unconstructed jackets.
- Shift, chemise, bias-cut A-line, flared, caftan and shirtwaist dresses.
- Flared, circle and straight-hanging dirndl skirts; stitched-down, flat-lying pleated skirts; full-cut split skirts; longer hemlines.
- Straight-leg and controlled pleat-front pants; palazzo pants and walking shorts slightly wider at the hem.
- Straight-hanging coats and capes.
- Layered looks.

Accessories
- Attention-getting pin or necklace.
- Scarves
- Mid to high heels and boots.

Avoid
- Emphasizing or exposing larger thighs with form-fitted clothes.
- Narrow shoulder lines.
- Totally plain bodices.
- Side zippers.
- Short jackets worn with straight skirts.
- Bulky bouffant, open pleat and pegged skirts; short hemlines.
- Bell-bottom, tapered and cuffed pants.
- Clingy or bulky fabrics.
- Horizontal lines in hip area.
- Tight, wide belts.
- Chunky shoes.

Larger Thighs at the Front

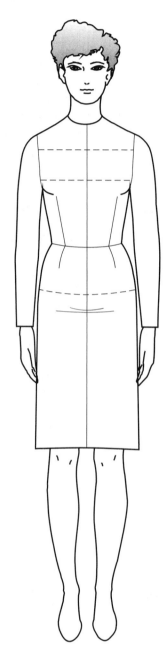

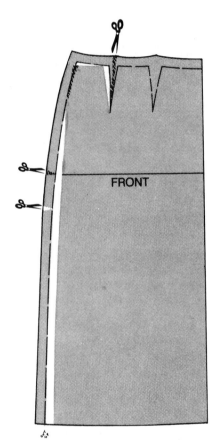

FRONT

Figure Variation
- Thigh muscles on the front of the leg are more fully developed than average.
- The groin area appears to indent more than average.

Fitting Problem
- There is not enough fabric width to fit across the front thighs.
- Fabric is tight across the upper front thighs.
- A horizontal fold may form just above the front thighs.
- Side seams are pulled forward at upper front thigh level.
- Fabric cups under the buttocks.
- Hemline may curve up at center front.

Fabric & Pattern Alteration
- The garment needs more fabric to fit around larger front thighs.
- Widen (let out) the garment front side seams from hem to full thigh level and taper into original seam at mid-hip.
- In pants, additional width on front side seams may also be tapered into original leg if preferred.
- In pants, widen the crotch extension and taper into original seamlines at mid-hip and at mid-thigh level.

Fashions to Fit & Flatter

General Guidelines
- Camouflage or draw attention up and away from larger front thighs to create the illusion of smaller front thighs.
- Clothes that require little or no alteration feature a loose, full fit below the waist.

Design Details & Specific Styling
- Interesting details in the neckline and shoulders.
- A-line, flared, and softly gathered dirndl skirts; full-cut split skirts.
- Full-cut slacks or shorts; multi-pleat-front pants and palazzo or pajama pants.

Accessories
- Medium belts.

Avoid
- Exposing or emphasizing large thighs in front with tight, form-fitting skirts, pants or shorts.
- Clingy or bulky fabrics.

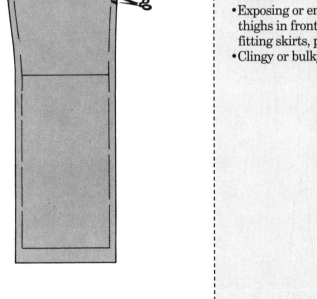

FRONT

Longer Legs

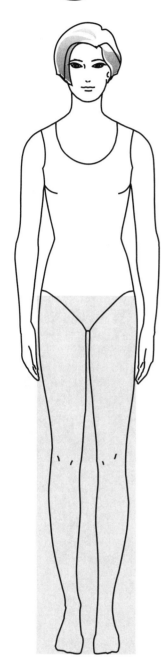

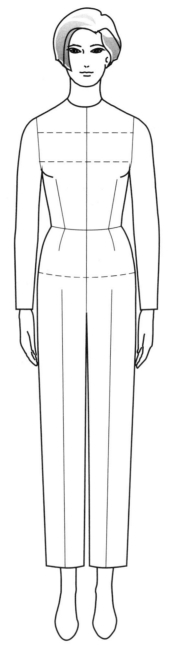

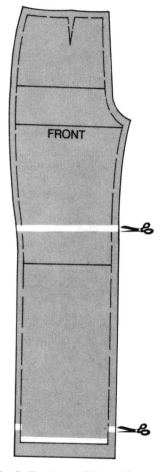

Figure Variation
- The leg bones are longer than average/ideal.
- Increased length can occur in the upper leg, lower leg or be distributed between both.
- Long legs can occur in combination with a short midriff or lower torso.

Fitting Problem
- There is not enough fabric length to cover the leg attractively.
- Garment flare or tapered shaping may be positioned too high on the leg.
- Hemline is positioned too high on the leg to appear proportionally attractive.

Fabric & Pattern Alteration
- The garment needs more length to position the hem at an attractive level on longer legs.
- Lengthen (let down) the garment evenly at the hem. Lengthen the pattern at approximately mid-thigh if necessary to retain styling.

Fashions to Fit & Flatter

General Guidelines
- Camouflage, balance or draw attention up and away from too long legs to create the illusion of shorter legs.
- Clothes that require little or hem alteration only, include skirts, jumpers, dresses and shorts.

Design Details & Specific Styling
- Interesting design details in the neckline and shoulders.
- Dropped waistlines.
- Below crotch-length tops, tunics, sweaters and jackets.
- Flared, bouffant and tiered skirts; skirts with godets; split skirt; skirts hemmed at mid-calf; trim at the hem if desired.
- Classic straight-leg slacks, pedal pushers, knickers, culottes, gauchos, and hip-huggers; cuffs on shorts and slacks.
- Flared, circle and swing-style coats, capes.
- Medium and heavier-weight fabrics.
- Horizontal stripes or line movement in skirts or pants; plaids and border prints.

Accessories
- Flats, low heels, ankle straps, T-straps.
- Boots over slacks; boot shoes and short boots.

Avoid
- Emphasizing proportionally too long legs with raised waistlines.
- Short tops; crop tops.
- Short vests, sweaters and jackets.
- Short or button-front skirts.
- Form-fitting pants.
- Vertical line movement in skirts and pants.
- Belts in same color as skirt or pant.
- High heels.

Special Note: Long legs are a fashion asset unless extreme or in proportion to a short torso. Enjoy!

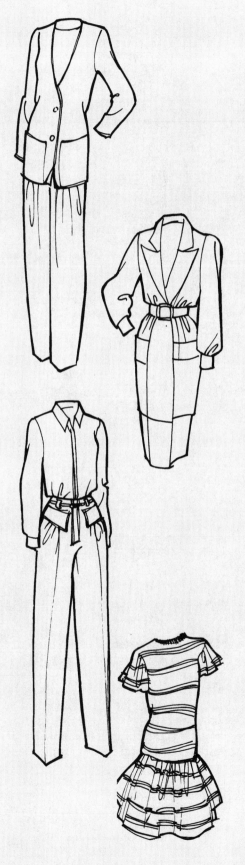

Shorter Legs

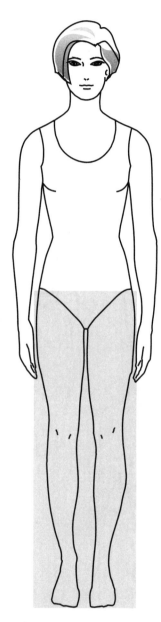

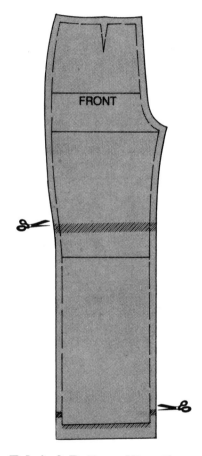

Figure Variation
- The leg bones are shorter than average/ideal.
- Decreased length can occur in the upper leg, lower leg or be distributed between both.
- Short legs can occur in combination with a long midriff or lower torso.

Fitting Problem
- There is too much fabric length to cover the leg attractively.
- Garment flare or tapered shaping may be positioned too low on the leg.
- Hemline is positioned too low on the leg to appear proportionally attractive.
- Fabric may cover the feet.

Fabric & Pattern Alteration
- The garment needs less fabric length to position the hem at an attractive level on shorter legs.
- Shorten (take up) the garment evenly at the hem. Shorten the pattern at approximately mid-thigh if necessary to retain styling.

Fashions to Fit & Flatter

General Guidelines
- Balance or draw attention up and away from shorter legs to create the illusion of longer legs.
- Clothes that require little or hem alteration only, include skirts, jumpers, dresses and shorts.

Design Details & Specific Styling
- Stand-up collars; high, narrow lapels.
- Shoulder details.
- Raised waistlines.
- Vertical slot or slash pockets.
- Shorter tops, vest, sweaters.
- Shorter jackets, including a bolero jacket.
- Empire, shift, chemise and princess line dresses.
- Straight, flared and gored skirts; and skirts pleated from the waist; skirts hemmed below the knee, below the calf, or to the floor; skirts with button front, front slit, or handkerchief hem.
- Classic straight-leg slacks, flared, palazzo, stirrup pants.
- Straight-hanging coats.
- Monochromatic, one color outfits—if desired.
- Light to medium weight fabrics in skirts and pants.
- Vertical stripes or line movement in skirts or pants.

Accessories
- Belts in color to match skirt or pant.
- Stockings to match skirt or pant, and shoe—if desired.
- Medium to higher heels in simple pump and sling-back styles.

Avoid
- Emphasizing shorter legs with dropped waistlines.
- Conspicuous hip pockets.
- Below crotch-length tops, vests, sweaters and jackets.
- Full bouffant and tiered skirts; ruffles or trim at the hem.
- Baggy, pegged or cuffed pants; pedal pushers, knickers and hip-hugger pants.
- Bulky, heavy, or textured fabrics in skirts and pants.
- Large-scale prints, and horizontal stripes or line movement in skirts or pants.
- Low-riding belts.
- Textured stockings or heavy socks.
- Stiletto high heels, chunky shoes, ankle straps, T-straps, bows at the instep and short boots.

Bowed Legs (Outward Knee Rotation)

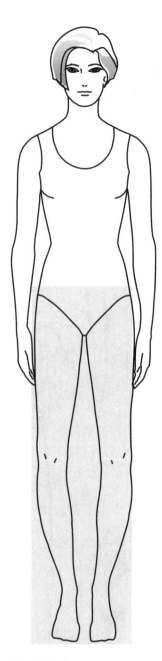

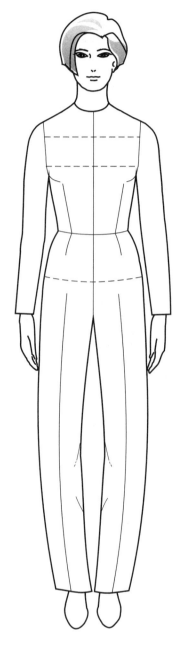

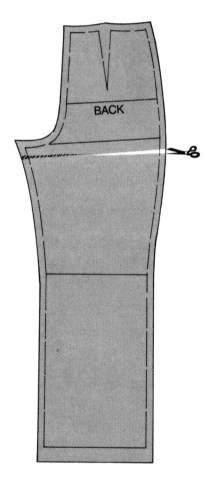

BACK

Figure Variation
- The leg bones bow outward.
- The greatest amount of curve may occur at the knee or the calf.
- Distance increases on the outside of the leg and decreases on the inside of the leg.
- Feet often turn inward to improve balance.

Fitting Problem
- This variation affects the fit of pants only.
- Crease lines follow the outward curve of the leg.
- Fabric may be strained along the outside seam and hang loose along the inside seam (inseam).
- Diagonal wrinkles may form across the inseam at the point of greatest curve.
- The hemline may rise at the sides.

Fabric & Pattern Alteration
- The garment needs more length on the outside seam and less length on the inside seam to fit the leg curve.
- Lengthen the outside seamline.
- Shorten the inside seamline.

Fashions to Fit & Flatter

General Guidelines
- Camouflage or draw attention up and away from bowed legs to create the illusion of straighter legs.
- Clothes that require little to no alteration include very full-styled pants and skirts.

Design Details & Specific Styling
- Details in the neckline and shoulders.
- Flared, dirndl, pleated and split skirts; skirts and dresses hemmed below the widest level of the bow.
- Flared pants.
- Dress-length coats.

Accessories
- Hats.
- Attention-getting earrings, pins and necklaces.
- Socks crushed down at the ankle.
- Flat to medium high heels; boots with longer skirts.

Avoid
- Exposing or emphasizing bowed legs with straight skirts and sheath dresses.
- Skirts and dresses hemmed above the bow.
- Tight-fitted, clingy pants and shorts.
- Very dark or light colored stockings with shorter skirts or pants.
- Ankle straps, T-straps and short boot shoes.

Knock Knees

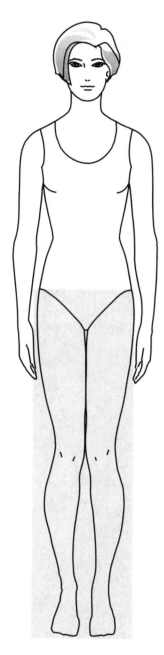

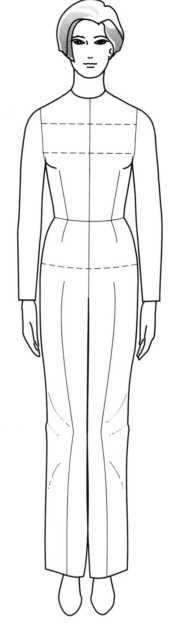

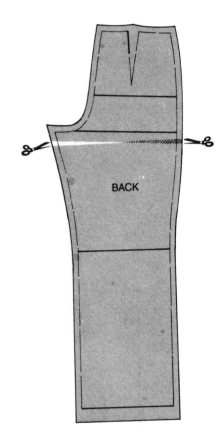

BACK

Figure Variation
- The leg bones angle inward at the knee.
- Distance increases on the inside of the leg and decreases on the outside of the leg.
- Feet often toe outward to improve balance.

Fitting Problem
- This variation affects the fit of pants only.
- The crease line follows the inward angle of the leg.
- Fabric may be strained at the knee along the inside seam (inseam) and droop loosely along the outside seam.
- Diagonal wrinkles may form across the outside seam at the knee and up.
- The hemline may rise at the inseam.

Fabric & Pattern Alteration
- The garment needs more length on the inside seam and less length on the outside seam to fit the leg curve.
- Lengthen the inside seamline.
- Shorten the outside seamline.

Fashions to Fit & Flatter

General Guidelines

- Camouflage or draw attention up and away from knock knees to create the illusion of straighter legs.
- Clothes that require little or no alteration include full-cut pants and skirts.

Design Details & Specific Styling

- Details in the neckline and shoulders.
- Softly styled skirts; split skirts; skirts and dresses hemmed well below the knees—below the calf where the angle becomes obvious; handkerchief hem.
- Flared or baggy pants, culottes, gauchos, palazzo and pajama pants, and sweatpants.
- Dress-length coats.

Accessories

- Hats.
- Attention-getting earrings, pins and necklaces.
- Socks crushed down at the ankle.
- Flat to medium high heels; boots with longer skirts.

Avoid

- Exposing or emphasizing knock knees with straight skirts and sheath dresses.
- Skirts and dresses hemmed near or above the knee; eye-catching trim at the hem.
- Tight-fitted, clingy pants and shorts.
- Very dark or light colored stockings with shorter skirts or pants.
- High heels, platform or chunky shoes, ankle or T-strap shoes.

Larger Legs

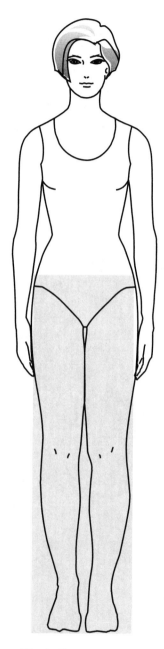

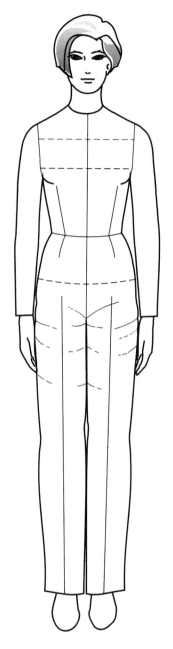

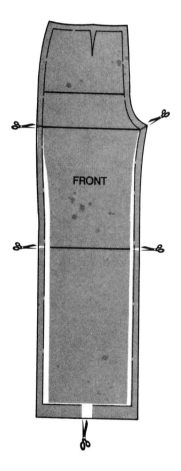

FRONT

Figure Variation
- The leg bones are larger or carry more weight than average/ideal.
- Weight can be deposited on the upper leg, lower leg, at the ankle, or be distributed evenly over the entire leg.

Fitting Problem
- There is not enough fabric width to fit comfortably and attractively around the leg.
- Tight, horizontal ripples or wrinkles can form around the leg.

Fabric & Pattern Alteration
- The garment needs more fabric width in the leg to fit larger legs.
- In skirts, see wide hips and large thighs at the outside.
- In pants, widen (let out) the garment at the sides, tapering into original seam at hipline.

Fashions to Fit & Flatter

General Guidelines
- Camouflage, balance or draw attention up and away from larger legs to create the illusion of slimmer legs.
- Clothes that require little or no alteration feature a loose, full cut in skirts and pants.

Design Details & Specific Styling
- Broad shoulder lines, epaulets and shoulder pads.
- Raised waistlines.
- Longer tops, sweaters, and jackets.
- Straight-hanging dirndl skirts; flared and gored skirts; flat-lying knife pleated skirts; hem two inches below the knee or below the widest part of the calf.
- Full-cut straight leg slacks and pleat-front pants; slightly flared, palazzo or pajama pants; pleat-front walking shorts, flared just above the knee.
- Dress-length coats.
- Lightweight layered looks.
- Darker colors in skirts and pants.
- Light to medium weight fabric in skirts and pants.
- Small-scale patterns and vertical stripes or line movement in skirts and pants.

Accessories
- Hats.
- Attention-getting earrings, pins and necklaces.
- Scarves

Avoid
- Exposing or emphasizing larger legs with straight, tight-fitting, pegged, box pleat or bouffant skirts; skirts hemmed above the knee or at the widest part of the calf; ruffles, scallops or trim at the hem.
- Knickers, jodhpurs, tight-fitting, tapered, pegged, and harem pants; bulky, conspicuous pockets; cuffs.
- Stretch, stiff, heavy, bulky, thick or textured fabric.
- Big, bold prints or plaids; horizontal stripes or line movement.

- White, opaque, patterned or textured stockings and bulky socks; dark stockings with light shoes.
- Dainty or platform shoes, ankle straps, T-straps, and short boots.

Thin Legs

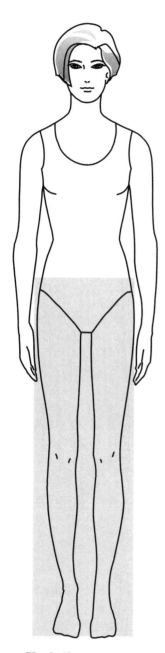

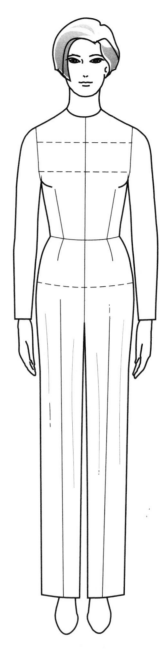

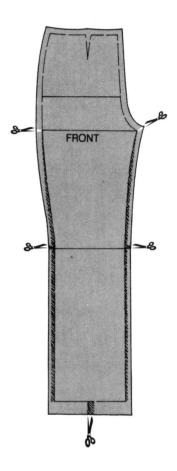

FRONT

Figure Variation
- The leg bones are smaller or carry less weight than average/ideal.
- Less weight can be deposited on the upper leg, lower leg, at the ankle, or over the entire leg.

Fitting Problem
- There is too much fabric width to fit comfortably and attractively around the leg.
- Loose, vertical ripples can form around the leg.

Fabric & Pattern Alteration
- Garment needs less fabric width in the leg to fit thinner legs.
- In skirts, see narrow hips.
- In pants, decrease garment width in the legs at the sides, tapering into original seam at hipline.

Fashions to Fit & Flatter

General Guidelines
- Camouflage, balance or draw attention up and away from thin legs to create the illusion of slightly heavier legs.
- Clothes that require little or no alteration feature soft styling in skirts and pants.

Design Details & Specific Styling
- Details in the neckline and shoulders.
- Skirts that are softly flared or gathered from the hip; a kilt or open-pleated skirt; skirts hemmed at mid-calf.
- Pleat-front pants, baggy, harem, palazzo, pajama and sweat pants; Bermuda shorts and cuffs.
- Textured fabrics, including corduroy and tweed.
- Horizontal stripes or line movement, and bold prints or plaids in skirts and pants.

Accessories
- Lightly textured or ribbed stockings, lightweight and crushed socks; leg warmers.
- Lightweight, eye-catching, strappy shoes; boots.

Avoid
- Exposing or emphasizing thin legs with extremely broad shoulder lines and shoulder pads.
- Straight, tight, short skirts; bouffant, tiered, or ruffled skirts.
- Knickers, pegged, tight or clingy pants and short shorts.
- Extremely bulky fabric.
- Vertical stripes or line movement in skirts and pants.
- Oversize, chunky or platform shoes and stiletto high heels.
- Dark stockings or tights and bulky socks.

Appendix

For further information on the figure variations presented in *Fabulous Fit*, refer to the following references in *Fitting & Pattern Alteration: A Multi-Method Approach*, by Elizabeth G. Leichty, Della N. Pottberg, Judith A. Rasband, also available throughFairchild Publications.

Figure Variation in Fabulous Fit	Fitting & Pattern Alteration Page Number
Bodices	
Larger, Thick Neck	212
Smaller, Thin Neck	214
Forward Neck (and Head)	216
Dowager Hump	218
Wide (Broad) Shoulders	222
Narrow Shoulders	226
Square Shoulders	230
Sloped Shoulders	234
Rounded Chest	250
Shallow Chest	252
Rounded Upper Back	254
Erect Upper Back	256
Wide (Broad) Chest/Upper Back	262
Narrow Chest/Upper Back	264
Larger Bust	284, 288
Smaller Bust	292
Longer Midriff/Low Waist	298
Shorter Midriff/High Waist	300
Larger Waist	130, 302
Smaller Waist	132, 304
Sleeves	
Longer Arms	314
Shorter Arms	316
Larger Arms	324
Smaller/Thin Arms	326
Larger Upper Arms	328
Inward Rotation of the Elbow	334
Skirts & Pants	
Longer Lower Torso	126
Short Lower Torso	128
Larger Abdomen	136
Flat Abdomen	138
Sway Back	140
Sway Front	144
High Hip Curve (Square)	146
Low Hip Curve (Sloped)	148, 190
Wide Hips	150
Narrow Hips	154
Larger Buttocks	166
Smaller/Flat Buttocks	170
Larger Thighs at the Outside	190
Larger Thighs at the Front	188
Longer Legs	180
Shorter Legs	182
Bowed Legs (Outward Knee Rotation)	192
Knock Knees (Inward Knee Rotation)	194
Larger Legs	198
Thin Legs	200

The following figure variations have few fashion limitations. Therefore they are not included in this book. They do, however, depend on good fit. Each variation and seam method of alteration is fully discussed in *Fitting & Pattern Alteration: A Multi- Method Approach*. References are listed below.

Index